What they don't tell you in college

What they don't tell you in college

How a new graduate can succeed in the workplace

Chris Payne

Illustrations by Ruperto Dela Cruz Jr.

First published by Lipa Publishing 2013
This paperback edition published 2016

Copyright © Chris Payne 2013-16
All rights reserved

No part of this book may be reproduced, stored in a retrieval system or transmitted by any means without the written permission of the author.

Unattributed opinions expressed in this book are entirely those of the author

ISBN 978-971-9678-00-7(Paperback)
978-971-9678-01-4(eBook)

Lipa Publishing
Helen Street,
Base View Homes
Lipa City, Batangas
The Philippines 4217

http://lipapublishing.com

Email: lipapub@yahoo.com.ph

The text is set in Arial font.

The photograph on page 2 shows some of the graduating class of 2009 at University College University of Maryland, reproduced with permission.

The Books of Chris Payne

Encounters with a Fat Chemist
Teaching at a University in Northern Cyprus

Balikwas
How to Emigrate to The Philippines

Java Quick and Easy

Self-Publishing Quick and Easy

<u>Fiction</u>

ERASED!

High Crimes and Low Stakes

The Descent of Gustave K

To Loydz, Jay and Apple

Contents

1 You need real-life skills….....   1
2 Starting out………………….   9
3 Getting a job……………….   25
4 Networking…………………..   49
5 The job interview…………….   57
6 Office politics……………….   81
7 Bosses……………………..   109
8 Meetings…………………….   119
9 Negotiating………………..   129
10 Changing your job…………..   139
11 Dressing for Success……...   151
12 Managing your money……..   161
Index

1 You need real-life skills

Congratulations new graduate !

Well done ! You are now a university graduate with letters after your name ! You have studied hard and listened to your professors who have nurtured your intellectual development. They will have been subject experts who will have told you all you need to know about computer programming or sociology or engineering. They will have given you, if you have paid attention to them, all the technical information you will need to start a fine career. Congratulations !

You are now an ace chemical engineer or a *summa cum laude* historian about to step up on to that stage to receive your diploma from some distinguished luminary in fancy robes.

The question now is, just how far is all that knowledge going to take you in the so-called 'real world' of work?

First, the real world is different. Let us assume that you do OK and you have the sort of career that millions of college graduates have. You may blunder into a career which more or less fits you and which you stick at for want of something better. You may move up the management ladder and, if you don't make too many serious career mistakes, you will slowly progress to a comfort level where you will come to rest.

What is absolutely certain is that you will never, over

your entire working life, spend very much time using all that subject knowledge so generously passed on to you by well-meaning professors. Instead, you will find yourself relying much more on practical life skills which we don't teach in college.

You are going to be spending a lot of time and mental energy on making your way in the world and earning a living. Success at doing that has little to do with whatever it says on your diploma. You are going to need more 'real-life' skills for success.

You are about to enter a highly competitive environment where you will be a first-day freshman once again. So enjoy your glorious Commencement moment in the sun. You worked for it and you've earned it ! Grown-up starts here.

Graduation is not the end of something –
It's the start of being grown up ! That is why
American colleges call it 'Commencement'

Money makes the world go round

So, what are they, these must-have skills which we don't bother to teach our young people? Well, first and foremost you will need financial skills. You will need to know how to handle money. We work for money. It is the way we feed ourselves and our families. It makes the world go round.

Everything runs on money. Money and the problems it brings are going to be a big worry for the new college graduate and, for that matter, the older college graduate too. Amazingly, we mostly still don't teach money skills to our young people. They are expected to pick them up by trial and error. Many a career has been wasted and many a life has been ruined because of ignorance about the mechanics of money.

Money has always had a bad press - the love of money is supposed to be the root of all evil. That is usually said by people who don't have too much of it or who find it difficult to hang on to. Money management is actually simpler than most of the things we tell our students, but we just don't explain it.

Well, that's not entirely true. We do make sure our trainees in economics and finance understand the mechanics of money. That is why they usually finish up having more money than, say, psychologists or historians or occupational therapists.

Nor do we give students much information about the relative financial rewards of different career paths. In this modern mercenary world, that is a shocking omission.

Time was when students could choose a line of work according to their fancy and be paid a middle class salary to do it. In those days, a university graduate, in whatever subject, could earn a good living, whatever their GPA or the class of their degree. Any old university degree could be cashed in for a decent job just about anywhere.

How quaint that sounds now, in an age when money is paramount and there are umpteen high-quality graduate applicants for jobs which used to be done by high school leavers.

Don't get me wrong. I am not suggesting that someone with a vocation for nursing or primary teaching should abandon their calling and study financial management. They might finish up being a rotten hedge fund trader instead of a great kindergarten teacher. It is just that such a student should be made aware of the financial implications of their choice, something we omit to mention in college. I just don't think it is right, in this day and age, that students should be let out into the world in a state of financial naiveté

Office politics are a fact of life

Then there are the office politics. After practical finance, office politics would be my second choice as a compulsory college course. Someone in a career, earning just enough to keep head above water, will spend almost as much time worrying about office politics as he/she spends worrying about money. Office politics is another thing we don't teach in college, or anywhere else, for that matter. In college, we never even mention it.

The newbie graduate is about to be thrown into shark-infested corporate waters full of credit-takers, back-stabbers, suckers-up and sundry devious schemers. We professors don't even tell them how to defend themselves against this army of fixers, chancers and other maladjusted souls.

Our babe in the woods may have come from a home and a high school where they were taught to play by the rules, always to tell the truth, never to cheat and always to be a 'nice guy'.

Then we send them into a jungle where nice guys finish last, if they finish at all. It is a place where there are no rules and certainly no merit badges or gold stars for being a decent human being.

It's a bit like putting your pet rabbit into the same cage as a herd (Is that the right collective noun?) of pythons.

We don't teach office politics anywhere. Since they are going to play such a large part in the professional life of the new graduate, that is not just neglectful, it is downright irresponsible.

I have written this book based upon more than just on fifty years of seeing students through to graduation. Over that time, I saw a pattern emerge. My student would pick up his diploma and then go off to some job or other to enjoy a promising future. Sometime down the line, usually after about two or three years, I would get a message from them asking for a letter of recommendation for a change of career direction.

I would, of course, write them up so as to give the subtle impression that they were the perfect human being – maybe an Einstein with the humanity of Saint Francis of Assisi and the vision of Martin Luther King. (One can't lay on the compliments too thick, in my experience.)

The student had actually possessed, in many cases, sufficient talent and intelligence to rise to the very top of their chosen profession - many less worthy human beings had gone on to achieve fame and riches.

Something had obviously gone wrong: something which happens in a lot of careers. It is even sadder than that if the victim only starts to realize they are making mistakes in their life when it is starting to get too late to correct them and when the youthful energy is starting to go.

Interaction with others, with all their flaws and hang-ups, was the real cause of my students' desires to cut their losses and try to make a fresh start. They had just not been prepared for the minefield that is career politics in the modern work environment.

Life is still survival of the fittest. We are civilized now so the struggle is not about risking life and limb as it was for our remote ancestors. But the same instincts are still there. These days we are more polite about it when we let them loose.

We don't teach a lot of other relevant but vital skills such as how to max your chances of getting the ace job or how to win arguments or how to negotiate for a promotion or a raise. We don't tell our student charges how to work a business meeting or how to network effectively or how to score at interviews.

Unlearning the old and learning the new

All is not lost if you have been misguided by well-meaning, but innocent, parents and school teachers. There are simple rules which will speed up the learning process and I have tried to summarize them here. They are certainly easier to understand than, say, differential equations or organic chemistry, subjects which you may have spent long hours studying at college.

In high school the student will have been taught how to be a good team player – how to work in a group and how to co-operate with others. Even in college, there will have been a support group you could rely to help you with the homework or to cover for you if you skipped a class.

The difference between college and the real world of work is that in the workplace you must work well with people you may not trust. They may even dislike you.

And, what is more, you will be on your own. Everything you do there will be down to you and to no one else. Self-reliance is probably the hardest lesson any of us ever has to learn.

If you are lucky, there will be a well-disposed mentor or patron who will guide you through the corporate jungle. It is much more likely though, that you will be thrown in at the deep end and you will have to learn the new rules for yourself.

Success and how to achieve it is not an unconscious process which one absorbs thoughtlessly as if by osmosis. If you have not made the progress you expected or what your professors led you to believe would be your due, or if all the glittering prizes have been given to someone else, it is not down to some invisible hand or the other guy's undeserved lucky break. It is because you don't know the rules. The good news is that the rules can be learnt.

Many of the points I make are from my own experience. Others are common knowledge, as written by a thousand organizational psychologists and management consultants in a million expensive textbooks and on a gazillion websites.

As a retired professor (IT and math, since you ask), I have a bad conscience about never having taught my students how to be corporate-savvy when I was in the classroom.

This small volume is a way of making amends, a modest offering to expiate my guilt at having behaved like many, if not most, unworldly college professors who concentrate on textbook information and ignore the real-life lessons for success.

There is only one way we learn anything and that is to copy someone who can already do what we need to know until we can understand and internalize the new knowledge. So it is with corporate survival. Keep your eyes and ears open because you have much to learn. I have written this book as a guide to shorten the length of the learning curve. Good luck !

2 Starting out

From college to the real world

Your twenties are a vital time in your life. They are the years when you move from child to full adult. At twenty life is to be lived for its enjoyments. You will probably still be in college and living the selfish life of what many adults would see as wild hedonistic pleasure. Of course there is study to do and exams to be passed but they are not usually too onerous.

The college life-style has to stop!

The party's over !

When it comes to your studies, you will already have figured out that a professor must set his tests at a level which the average student i.e. you, can pass easily. He can't set absolute standards because, as you, the student, will have realized, he cannot fail too many of his class if he wants to keep his job.

Then there are the new excitements of living away from home, and of meeting new and interesting friends and lovers.

The life of a twenty-year-old student has its various problems, of course, but Mom and Dad may still be there in the background to fund the experiment of entering adulthood and to provide a haven in the parental home when the problems do crop up. They will be only too happy to take care of them for you.

By thirty, the landscape will have changed completely. You may be stuck in a job which you may hate or adore. There could well be a significant other and you may be in a permanent relationship. You may be a parent. There will probably be debts and financial problems and you could be working somewhere which is a malign warzone of office politics. If it is not a warzone, then, at the very best, it will still be a place where you will need to tread carefully.

Between those two milestones, there is much to do in the way of mental readjustment. What is more, the time between those significant birthdays is a lot shorter than you think. As any older person will tell you, time passes more quickly as it goes by.

Many treasured ideas inherited from childhood will need to be dumped and replaced by something more realistic. You will learn, in those ten years that your teachers and parents were not infallible. You will, if you are sensitive enough, realize that those early role models had themselves been under life pressures which may have led them to pass on to you, unconsciously, life lessons that were just plain wrong.

Let us start with some simple and obvious things you need to clear about. They are not a way of life, even less a philosophy. They are just some basic facts which it makes sense to absorb before you are thrown out into the cold, hard world beyond Commencement.

Ten years on and your life will have changed !

Ten things you will need to know

1 You will never be rich and you will not win the lottery

Are you going to be rich? No, almost certainly not. True, there are a lot, well thousands, of millionaires who have made themselves rich. But as a proportion of the population they are a pretty small bunch. Their talent for getting rich is not shared by most of the seven billion souls who inhabit this planet.

And as for making really big money, really humungous money, like the sort of money Warren Buffet has or Richard Branson has, well, that requires a very special talent indeed. Those people make money effortlessly the way ordinary folks breathe.

Unfortunately for most of us, the Midas touch which those individuals possess is a gift conferred on very few exceptional people. They may not even know how they do it, any more than a great concert pianist can explain how she can play the trickiest piece of music perfectly.

Who knows, you might tell yourself, I might win the lottery or get some other windfall. No you won't. No one wins the lottery. Well, obviously someone does but it won't be you so don't waste your money buying a ticket. The lottery is just a scam to make people pay voluntary taxes. In the

United Kingdom where I used to live, the odds of winning the National Lottery in any one week, big enough to make a difference to your life, are about fourteen million to one against.

Let me write that as a decimal. Yes, each week, the probability of a life-changing win in the UK lottery is 0.000000071 That is pretty tiny. It is what your math professor would call 'vanishingly small' i.e. zero. Those odds are significantly worse than the chance of being killed by lightning in any single year which are about one in 300,000. In fact, don't gamble at all. The English call it a 'mug's game'.

2. You will not become famous as a movie/sports star.

Wouldn't it be nice to be famous as a star of the soccer pitch or the silver screen? It won't happen. Two reasons. One is simple luck, and you don't have it. 'I might be lucky' is the perpetual cry of the gambler-loser. You don't 'get lucky' - no-one does.

Here's a little mental exercise. Just think of exactly how many times in your life you could have had what you might really call 'a lucky break'. How many? One, two? Yep, that's right, the fingers of one hand or less.. Luck, in the sense of being smiled on by some generous, benevolent angel, just doesn't exist.

The uncomfortable fact is that for every Julia

Roberts or Cristiano Ronaldo there are a thousand hopefuls who are good, yes, really very, very good indeed. They are probably much better than you are but even they just don't quite cut it. They lack the crucial last 0.0001% of talent or beauty which separates the winner who gets showered with millions from the also-rans who get nothing at all.

Forget about fame, it is a mirage. Andy Warhol was dead wrong. Almost every single person in the world never comes anywhere near fifteen minutes of fame. Not even fifteen nanoseconds.

3. You will not come up with some great new idea

Microsoft *Windows* made Bill Gates the world's richest man but that was then and he just happened to be in the right place at the right time at the start of the computer revolution. But for every Bill Gates there are another million inventors with great ideas which will never leave their garage or bed-sitter.

It is also a myth that the Internet revolution presents unlimited opportunities for innovation. In fact, the digital revolution is already over and we are living in its aftermath. There will still be new e-businesses starting up from time to time but, overall, the Internet business world is a jungle with few survivors. The casualty rate for e-businesses is very high. It is reported that 80% of

Internet start-up businesses fail in the first year.*

It is a fact that everyone has brilliant ideas on a regular basis, ideas which could get them proclaimed a genius if those brainwaves ever saw the light of day. The reason they wither on the vine is because genius is only 1% inspiration. The other 99% is perspiration. Most people lack the persistence to develop their great sparks of genius. Anyway, if you were going to be a successful start-up entrepreneur, you wouldn't be reading this book now.

4. Your education and talent are not enough on their own to make you successful.

You may be the smartest kid in your class and you may walk away with the best degree which your elite Ivy League college has ever offered but that is no guarantee of landing the job you really want. It helps, of course, but as least as important as academic prowess are everyday talents like being willing to work hard or to understand how human relationships work in a political environment like an office.

Personality, social skills and being able to see the big picture of the business are often more valuable to an employer than your *summa cum laude* diploma.

You are going to have to learn how to be a hard-working obedient employee with good

---
*Quoted on 'Click', BBC News 31 January 2015

manners, tenacity, persistence and adaptability.

If you are indeed the star graduate of your year, it is very likely that you will have spent many years listening to a mantra which goes something like *'education, education, education, you can't have too much education'*. If that was your experience, then it will have been easy to get the idea that a good education is all it takes to make a successful life.

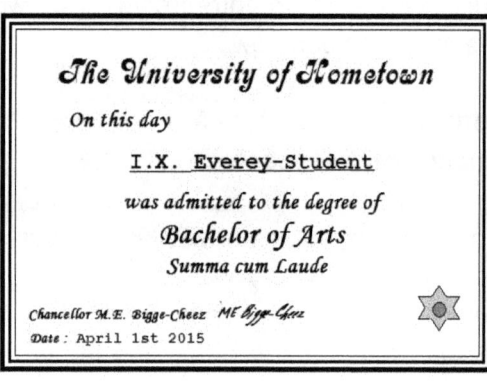

***A college diploma is nice to have
but it's not enough on its own.***

The world is full of people whose only single important moment was that afternoon when they picked up their college diploma from some semi-famous Commencement speaker. Mediocrity and obscurity beckon for those who put all their faith in that single piece of paper.

The real winners in life are more often the street-wise or the smooth operators whose scholastic record is more ordinary. But if you have both – a great academic record and social/political skills to match, then I look forward to seeing you on the cover of *Time* magazine.

5. You cannot spend all your income because you think you will have time enough to make money when you are older

When you start earning your own money, there is a tendency to blow the whole lot. Is life not expensive for young graduates at the foot of the salary ladder? What does it matter, you might tell yourself, if you spend up by the end of the month? Retirement, at the other end of your life, is such a long way away. You still have plenty of time to take care of paying for it in those long high-earning decades which lie ahead – your thirties, forties and fifties.

Do not be seduced by this false argument. From the moment you begin your first proper job, you need to start building up a cushion of money to protect yourself against those problems which are waiting for you – illness, getting fired, car repairs, whatever.

Or you might want to get married and have children, two events which do not come cheap. If you do become a parent, there will be college fees on the horizon. What do you mean 'that's over twenty years in the future'? Twenty years is a very short time, as we have already said.

6. You should not try to make a career of a personal interest unless you are very, very good at what you do.

A basic rule is that if you are sufficiently good at something, something which is your passion, then the money will appear. This might seem to be condoning you spending your life doing something you really enjoy, like acting, or rock music. It all depends on how good you are. The operative word is 'sufficiently'. Many lives have been ruined by students trying to get into a way of life because they would be doing something which had always been a favourite hobby. Hobbies are for amateurs and amateurs are people who do something for nothing because they are not good enough to get paid for it.

So, if that is the way you are intending to go, be sure you know how good you are. Parental applause when you play the saxophone has nothing to do with whether you can hack it as a professional musician.

We all change our interests as we get older and what floats your boat at twenty looks like adolescent self-indulgence when you are forty. If you are among the very best at your chosen *metier*, by which I mean being, possibly, in the top 0.01% in your state, then sure, try to make a living from it.

But if you are just 'following your heart', always keep in mind that you still have to earn a living, preferably a living as comfortable as possible.

If you only realize your mistake when you are a few years out of college, then all your fellow students from your graduating class will have several years start on you. What is more, you will not be as attractive to an employer who will now have any number of fresh new graduates to choose from.

7. Your health will not take care of itself

Your health is one of your most precious assets and like all precious assets it needs to be protected and cared for. At college you can party all night and still be fit to go to next morning's nine o'clock lecture on calculus or economic theory.

By the time you are thirty, you will need your rest and recovery. The wild parties, the smoking, the drinking, the weed and the sexesses can no longer be kept up. Get serious ! The world of work is a competitive arena where fitness is essential for the battle.

8. You must learn not to give up when the going gets tough

You are going to suffer some setbacks during your life. It is never going to be a bed of roses. There will be major disappointments. Maybe, if you are particularly unfortunate, there even may be personal tragedies.

We all read about someone else's misfortunes or we see them on TV with its prurient close-up's of tearful victims. Our normal response is to tell ourselves that such will not happen to us. To comfort ourselves, we pretend that those things only happen to other people.

Every single one of us will experience setbacks and losses as we go through life. One must learn, after one leaves the protective insulation of college, to be strong in the face of adversity.

When you get fired, or your business goes into bankruptcy, you must learn to acquire the strength to rebuild and start again. This can be a very difficult life lesson if you are going to survive those future setbacks which will certainly recur during your life. Mental toughening up is essential for the fully-formed adult.

9. You should never think that moving to a new place will make things better

There is a temptation, when things are going badly, to believe that salvation will be found in a new location. This could be a new job or a new house in a different part of the country. Few problems are so difficult that a drastic change of that kind is the only solution. If you are offered a game-changing promotion somewhere else, then taking it makes perfect sense. But changing location or job because of some indistinct feeling of discontent is a very stupid idea.

There are people who move house every few years for no discernible reason, even though they will rationalize to themselves what they are doing. They constantly see greener grass everywhere else. In actuality, people who go for regular aimless changes of job or location probably have something lacking in their lives. Better than moving would be to try to analyze the situation to get to the source of the problem. Then work on changing that, if possible.

The author Malcolm Gladwell* came up with a theory that it takes roughly ten thousand hours of practice (i.e. approximately five years of 40-hour working weeks) to achieve mastery in any field, including your work skills. The flipside of this is that if you are continually chopping and changing, then you will never have enough time to develop the skill which will earn you your living..

10. You will need to learn good time-management habits

I once worked for a school which worked eight-week terms and I would sometimes set a 4000 word term paper at the start of term. Now, eight weeks divided into 4000 words means writing 500 words a week. But that is not what the

---

*http://en.wikipedia.org/wiki/Outliers_(book)

students did. Many of them left writing of the paper until the day before it was due to be handed in. Then they would scribble all 4000 words at once.

Quite often they were late handing it in and would plead pressure of work. Naturally, because the work had been rushed, it was invariably of poor quality or, worse, copied from another student. That is why many a potential A-student finished up getting C's. and D's.

No matter how many times I remonstrated with them and advised them of the benefits of scheduling their time properly, few of them felt any pressure to follow my advice. 'Look', I would tell them, 'treat college as you would a job and put in a regular 40-hour week.'

Unlike real-life work where indolence will be quickly punished, there are no college penalties if you are lazy, just as long as you are doing enough to get by.

If you want to succeed in any part of life, you must learn to prioritize and schedule your work load. Keep a diary and an appointments book. There is one on your computer. List all your obligations and keep it properly updated.

Prioritize all the jobs you have to do and make estimates of the time you should apportion to each. Allow a margin for time overruns. Writing this to-do list should be one of the first things you do every morning when you start work.

When you are given a new job to do, try to do

it straight away, unless you are in the middle of something more important.

The aim of time management is to give you extra time to do more and thus gain a reputation for competence.

If you manage your time efficiently, you will be able to take on more tasks and if you do more work then you will be of greater value to your employer.

You do not have to be a 'multi-tasker' but you will find, if you get into good time-management habits, they become part of your personality. You will learn how to multi-task naturally.

You will become the sort of person who can be relied on to complete the jobs which have been allocated to you. People will bring you work because they know you will do it properly. Word will get around and your reputation as a winner will spread.

When I was a college professor, I noticed that it was those students who learned to make the fullest use of their time who got the top grades. I could never quite understand why students were happy with poor grades because they had left homeworks and term papers until the very last minute. Doesn't everyone want to be a success in life?

Successful people realize that time is infinitely precious. Losers just say 'mañana'.

Manage your time, make yourself efficient and indispensable if you want to succeed.

3 Getting a job

Work is a fact of life

We all have to work. We might not like it but we have to make the best of it.

It has always seemed to me that most of us have a choice when it comes to the work we finish up doing. We can be well paid and then we can be either happy or miserable or we can be badly paid which means we will certainly be miserable. Money does not guarantee happiness but poverty sure guarantees misery.

Of course, some lucky few don't need to work. They are born with a silver spoon and whether they spend their lives idly or productively is no more than a personal choice.

I like the story about the late Senator Edward Kennedy when he was a young politician on the campaign trail. A construction worker shouted to him 'Mister Kennedy, they say you never had a job in your life. Well, lemme tell you something. You ain't missed a thing !'

Most of us are not so fortunate and we need to get money to live by. The more we get, the higher our standard of living. For most of us, the only way to get money is to get a job. Yes, I know this is all blindingly obvious but it's amazing how many people forget this simple fact of life. They think, those people, that everything will turn out OK because it always has so far while they were being cared for and looked after in the family home. They think that putting time and effort into getting the best job they can find is not very important. A person like that is not leading their life, it is leading them.

The basic fact is that you are not going to survive without an income and unless you have family money or you want to live on begging or social security, then a job is what you need. And that job has to be the best-paying job you can find.

So, let's face it, for the average person, apart from becoming a professional criminal or marrying money, the only way you are going to survive is to become a wage slave. Marrying for money is a possibility, of course, but it is probably more difficult to pull off than it looks in those rom-com films. If you can hook up with the offspring of a billionaire then well done, good for you. You can stop reading now.

And as for becoming a professional criminal - a suave cat burglar, perhaps, or maybe a stylish Robin Hood figure, like the boys in *Ocean's Eleven* - is probably a very hard way to make a living. It is certainly a vocation which requires much more talent than slotting into life as a salaryman.

So don't despair at becoming a wage-slave. It could be far worse – you could be a no-wage slave. Let's try to leverage the odds to make you a wage-slave winner. The big problem is that first 'real' job, not just burger flipping or waitressing.

Job competition is fierce these days, so the problem needs to be approached on more than one front. There are a number of ways of getting into gainful employment and you have a better chance of getting the dream job if you can work them all.

There will be others who are more and less attractive to an employer than you are. But, the good news is that all those millions of new graduates who join the job market every summer are equally unknown quantities with no track record. This means that an employer has to rely on instinct and the applicant's presentation when it comes to choosing who to employ. You must work to make yourself the most attractive candidate by your personal presentation.

Job adverts

The traditional way is to apply for a job you have seen advertised in a newspaper or a trade journal. This is always a long shot. You get sent, or these days you download, an application form which demands a full biography describing every minute of your life from birth onwards.

Then the form goes back to the company advertising the job, or more likely to some recruitment agency which is handling the process on its behalf. You will be asked to send all sorts of supporting material such as a résumé (or CV) plus testimonial letters, college transcripts, photographs, diplomas and maybe a lot more besides. It is a tiresome business.

People have got jobs this way but, in my experience, the hit rate is very much less than 1% which translates into one job per hundred applications.

Answering lots of job adverts is not for the faint-hearted

I always reckoned that I would need to send ten applications to get an acknowledgement and ten or twenty acknowledgements before I got an interview.

If you do get a job this way, of course, you can always say you've been 'head-hunted'. Indeed, you will have beaten some very long odds.

If the hiring company is using a recruitment agency, that fact alone gives the game away. Most companies only have small HR (Human Resources) departments and coping with the vast volume of applications is usually too much for them, so they out-source the work to an agency.

A friend of mine was a college librarian in a small town. When he advertised for an entry-level trainee librarian, he got 1200 applications. Every HR department and recruitment agency in the world has similar tales to tell.

Getting a good testimonial or reference

Here is one tip I have found useful. Get recommendation letters from the most important, prestigious people you know. Not your professor, of course, or his boss. No, go to the president of the university and ask him to write you a letter of recommendation. Will he do it? No, you bet he won't and neither will his provost or the dean.

Your requests will get passed down the line to your professor - by which time your letter or email may just have disappeared into the trash can or cyberspace.

Here's what to do instead. Write the letter of recommendation yourself because the president is too busy ! You are presenting the great man with a problem but you are also presenting him with a quick ready-made solution !

It is an infallible rule that very important, very busy people do not like to be given problems. If you do take a problem to him/her then they always appreciate it if you also take them the solution.

So, giving your self-recommendation the OK is quicker for him than passing it on to his second in command. All you need from him is a signature. He might not pass it unchanged of course – he might feel honor bound to make a few minor cosmetic changes for form's sake. But they will be minimal.

You can then get your testimonial without causing the president more than a minute's brain time. Then he can forget about you forever. Just make sure that the president's name appears prominently in your application's covering letter.

Why, you may ask, should the president of your college bother doing this for you? Well, like all college presidents he wants to feel that he is in touch with his students. Even though he doesn't know most of them from Adam, he still likes to think of himself as the patriarch of the college 'family'.

Filling out the application form

When you fill out an application form, it is vital that you follow the instructions on layout *etc.* to the letter. This is important because anyone sifting through ten thousand applications will need a reason, any reason, not to read almost all of them. Only the absolutely perfectly presented application will get through the first round when 99% or more will be discarded.

A form where a single answer spills over the edge of the box will be thrown away unread. If you use blue ink when the form specifies black, your application will not even be looked at. What employer will want to employ someone who can't follow simple instructions?

Another thing you might do is to type the application if the instructions invite you to. Hand-written forms, even those perfectly filled in with the finest calligraphic copperplate script may also be discarded straight off.

The job of the recruiting agency is to present a dozen, maybe twenty, or so completed forms to the company HR department for the final shortlist. Those few may not be the best applicants out of the ten thousand who applied but they are good enough, and, what is more, they can follow simple instructions regarding form filling.

These days it is the Internet where job applications are usually made. This lengthens the odds, since every Tom, Dick or Harry can now apply. Where once applications came in by the hundreds or the thousands, the Internet means that advertisements for desirable jobs now attract millions of hopefuls. Obviously, even more stringent filtering out must be applied.

One filter used at this level is where you live. We may be living in a global world with a *World Wide Web* but it is only worth local residents applying for local jobs. Employing expatriates, even for online jobs, involves all sorts of problems with visas, taxation, immigration rules, foreign bank accounts and so on. Companies can also save on interview expenses by simply not reading applications sent from the other side of the country.

Over time, you will build up a standard pack of all the required documentation. If you have the copies of all this material ready to send, then the process is reduced to filling up a new form each time and emailing it.

Unfortunately, the odds against success are so long

that urban folklore is full of stories of people who send off tens of forms every day for months on end before they get anywhere near the sniff of a real job.

Wry comments along the lines of 'My full-time day job is filling up application forms' feature regularly on the job-hunters' blogs.

Blind job applications are like cold calling. The chances of making a sale i.e. getting a job, are very, very poor but slightly, only very slightly, better than not applying at all. There must be a more efficient way of doing it, surely? Yes, there is.

The personal touch

The answer is using personal contacts, by far the best way to secure gainful employment. During your college career you should start building up a network of good contacts. You need to work on developing a serious address book. If you are at a top school like Oxford or Harvard, then your contacts are likely to move on to useful influential positions. So make sure you stay friends with them. Don't steal their girlfriends and don't cry if they steal yours. This is business and business does not have emotions.

Identify the useful people among your contemporaries and cultivate them. Flatter them. Send them birthday greetings, stand them drinks, write about them admiringly in the student magazine. Treat them as if they will one day be writing your pay check because they just might be.

So, how do you identify those who are going to have a great future and those who are just sounding off?

At the college level, tomorrow's success story is very likely the sort of person who gets things done quietly. Avoid the loudmouth who tells you how great he's going to be. Ten years down the road he will be a middle school English teacher reading *Pride and Prejudice* to bored 13 year olds.

No, tomorrow's go-getter is just passing through college on his way to bigger things, so he doesn't have time for unnecessary grandstanding. Cultivate him and any others like him although you should beware if they tell you they have a grand plan for getting rich quickly. If they do then they are not being realistic.

Network widely, not just at college and not just in your preferred line of work. (See Chapter 4) Even if you know what your dream job is then you will be competing with lots of other talented kids who also see it as their dream job. You may even be outstanding when it comes to the job requirements but it is an unfortunate rule of life that no-one is number one for long. There is always someone who is better than you are.

So working through your contacts for the dream job may work but likely it may not. Lots of others are doing exactly the same thing. So if another offer comes along, which is not quite what you want and is not as good as you would like, then take it.

It is always easier to get a job if you already have a job. The big deal is getting the first job, getting one's foot in the door. As long as it is a 'real' job, not just serving fast food, you are on your way.

How to write a great résumé

You are going to need a well-written résumé (or CV if you are European). It is what the potential employer is going to use to decide whether to call you for interview or not, so it should be a high-quality work of art. It should be well-written, beautifully presented and just concise enough to be read quickly. The data on your résumé should include :

> ***Contact information*** – name, address, email, website, phone numbers;
> ***Accomplishments and achievements*** – the most recent first;
> ***Career narrative*** – make it an interesting read. It should be a well-phrased concise statement about your ambitions and your skills;
> ***Relevant URL's*** where you have been involved such as links to your work;
> ***'Metrics'*** These are measurable achievements e.g. position in class, charity funds raised, number of visitors to your website etc. Include anything which can be measured because recruiters prefer hard numerical information over self-centered waffle.

The employer is not going to be interested in what you were doing ten years ago. He wants to know what you are doing now. If you are applying for your first job, then your résumé should show evidence of your scholastic successes and your out-of-school interests but only where these are relevant. If you do serious voluntary charity work you can put that in but if your off-duty time is spent hanging out with Hell's Angels, then certainly don't mention it. In fact, it is better not to say anything about your non-professional interests because they are of no interest to anyone but you. For example, if you spend a lot of time singing in the church choir or playing in a rock band, don't mention it. It won't help your cause. It may even alienate a potential employer, especially if he's an atheist who hates rock music.

And that's about it for the first-timer. As you get older, the résumé will get fatter as you add more to it. But the recent graduate should try to keep it down to no more than two sides of A4 paper, preferably just one.

Layout and appearance are critical for instant impact. Use a serious, not decorative, font such as Tahoma, Calibri or Verdana. Times New Roman is a little old hat these days – clean, neat, sanserif fonts are better. Never mix fonts on the same document.

The word processor has made the production of high quality printed documents available to everybody, so making your résumé stand out from all the others involves a lot of polishing.

When you have written it, make sure you run it through the spell checker several times until you are absolutely sure that there are no spelling or grammatical errors. Then ask a friend or your college professor to proof read it for accuracy and consistency and for the tone you are trying to project.

A single typo or inaccuracy will be noticed instantly. Just the one will give the immediate impression of slapdash carelessness. However insignificant the error may seem, it may be enough to cost you the job. The résumé is going to be your main item of self-advertising material so make sure that it is PERFECT !

An article in Britain's *Independent* newspaper* revealed that the average résumé is read in 8.8 seconds! A high proportion of résumés can be rejected out of hand because, as many recruiters will tell you, too many of today's résumés show one or more of the following faults:

1 Bad grammar
2, spelling mistakes
3. Missing or incorrect information
4. Poor design e.g. with an unusual font style or size
5. The résumé is too long or too short
6. The tone is too casual or informal.
7. The applicant has used jargon
8. The exam gradeshave been listed in full detail
9. Irrelevant out-of-date information e.g kindergarten grades, has been included
10. Listing of generic interests e.g.reading or cooking
11 There is too much irrelevant personal information
12 The applicant included an image of themselves.

You may be the exact fit for the job but the recruiter does not know that. If you make a single one of these mistakes, your application will be trashed in just a few seconds.

---

* Independent London 20th January 2015
  http://www.independent.co.uk/news/uk/home-news/employers-sifting-through-applications-likened-to-swiping-through-tinder-as-research-shows-people-spend-88-seconds-looking-at-a-cv-9988512.html

A recruiter spends less than 8.8 seconds reading your résumé

Planning your career

It is a good idea to make a plan of your intended career path for about ten years ahead. Identify where you want to be a decade on and work back to plot how you are going to get from here to there. We can't define the means unless we first define the end.

So, the first job may not appear to be going in the right direction. For example, you may want a job in high finance and find that you can only get a job in a retail store. So how do you get from A to B?

Well, retail stores have finance departments and your first move should be to aim to get a transfer there. Then make new contacts in retail finance and use them to get where you want to go by moving crabwise, sideways, until you feel you are on the right track.

A job on Wall Street may be your ideal final destination and for the moment it may be unattainable. Less glamorous working environments such as retailing or the hotel industry are easier to get into. What is more, they pay well and there are opportunities for travel and making new useful contacts. Entry into those professions is less likely to depend on which school or college you went to.

I chose the example of the retail store deliberately. One of my former students did just that. Her interests are in high finance but she could only get her first job as a sales assistant in a women's clothing store. But after two or three well-planned moves over a few years, she is now a corporate strategy analyst with a major international bank.

Job opportunity areas

You could try looking for job opportunities in less attractive parts of the world. Some parts of Europe and North America are suffering depopulation and they do not have the amenities and the attractions of the big cities. These areas include, for example, the Northern

US Midwest states. But there are big mining and engineering companies working there which provide well-paid job opportunities.

For example, the United States has recently moved its energy policy towards more emphasis on home-grown supply and that creates a whole shed-load of opportunities.

A foot in the door in a North Dakota mining or water company could be the first step in a great career. This might seem to violate a basic money rule that to make money you have to be physically near where the money is. (See Chapter 12) But remember, those companies pay well and they have senior positions filled by internal promotion.

Big mining companies may have field operations in cold, desolate and hostile places that no one wants to go to but they also have their corporate headquarters where the big money hangs out, like Wall Street or the City of London.

At this moment, the IT industries are where the main action is. Companies like *Google, Amazon* and *Facebook* are making millions and many people who invested in them or took jobs with them ten years ago have done well. But that will not last forever – even the hottest, most original, big IT company will eventually mature into a safe blue-chip stock. A good example is IBM which was once the Apple of its day.

The rate of innovation in computer applications has probably already passed its peak. When everyone has a SmartPhone or a laptop, it is safe to assume that IT, as an industry, is now on a plateau. Future opportunities are going to come along much more slowly than they have in the last twenty years.

If you are ambitious, your focus needs instead to be on what is likely to be still in its growth phase ten years from now. That will be about the time when you will be approaching your own peak.

Look out for new developments and economic trends. Keep reading the business press to try to spot the next big thing. It need not be high-tech. To give just one example, there has been a significant recent change in American policy with regard to the way American industries have outsourced low-tech manufacturing these last thirty years. There is evidence that these jobs are returning home after decades in the Far East. Just as in the energy industry mentioned above, there has been a sea-change in American business which is turning the economy back to home-made. The last tidal change, when the economic mood was for enthusiastic outsourcing, happened during the Reagan era, thirty years ago. The pendulum is swinging back. You can safely assume that this current change of direction will also be long-term and could coincide neatly with your own career.

Another area to look at is engineering, which is not considered glamorous but which is currently undergoing something of a renascence. All over the western world, and especially in the US, people are becoming aware of the need to invest more, much more, in long-neglected infrastructure. The investment is likely to be so large, that there will be openings, not just for engineers but for all subject majors.

Develop a careful long-term career plan

Working at a start-up company

Most start-ups do not survive – there is always a large attrition rate for all new companies. However, if the business plan is not too off-the-wall, you might be able to buck the odds and get in on the ground floor of something gigantic.

I always remember a valuable learning mistake I made when I was eighteen. I was fresh out of high school and, having nothing else to do one afternoon, I filled in an application form for a job with a small start-up company. The interview was in a 10' x 12' office which had one desk and a filing cabinet.

I was interviewed by one of the two partners – the other was out on the road – and he offered me a job which I turned down because I didn't see myself in their line of work as the third and junior member of a property company. Besides, I wanted to go to college.

How stupid of me ! Fast-forward twenty years and those two partners had become the multi-millionaire owners of the largest chain of estate agents in the North of England and they were watching the start of a ten year property boom.

I made all the mistakes.

Internships

If you get a chance, work some internships during your long summer vacations. Internships are working for nothing so if you are in need of money, you may also need to take a paying job in a bar or restaurant during the evenings.

The main thing about an internship is not the learning on the job because the company is unlikely to be very interested in you or your future. Being an intern today is not unlike being an apprentice in the nineteenth century, who would have to pay the employer for the privilege. The only difference is that if you are an intern for a large company these days, you don't also get presented with a bill for your training. The thinking is that the intern is being paid sufficiently in experience gained and for the right to put the company's name in the student résumé.

Most employers treat interns like free casual labor, which, of course, is exactly what they are. Do not baulk at that. You are not working as an intern for them; the reason for their existence is to provide you with valuable contacts and connections.

Be sure to have business cards ready when business customers come to call. In fact, it is a good idea never to leave home without at least twenty cards. Sprinkle them around like confetti to visitors to the office. Sooner or later you will connect with someone. Have a few copies of the résumé nearby, should you get into conversation with a possible lead.

The great thing about an internship is that it doesn't come with any baggage about 'loyalty'. Since they haven't been paying you, any loyalty in the deal should have come from them.

Using your family connections

If you are lucky, you will have family connections. Prince Charles will never have to take a Head of State interview and George W. Bush would probably never have become President of the USA if he had had to apply for the job via an online application form.

But even for lesser mortals there are family connections which can be very useful. Uncle Mort's Hardware Store for example. Can you really put hand on heart and swear that you did everything you could to become his favourite niece or nephew even before he got his dodgy ticker?

Even if you don't have any immediate family business connections, the six-degrees-of-separation theory means that your close relatives may only be a friend-of-a-friend away from the person you really need to get to know.

Never undervalue yourself

The failing of a lot of new job seekers is that they display false modesty. It is a most unattractive personal quality. Unfortunately, it is encouraged in grade school where they teach you that you should never be seen to be 'blowing your own trumpet' or 'sucking up'.

Remember, schools are more concerned with turning out nice, well-adjusted, obedient citizens (The shorthand term is 'losers'.) than helping those students get on in the world. Unfortunately this means teaching some harmful attitudes and one of them is false modesty which is encouraged in young people lest they become conceited, which is 'not nice'.

The successful person knows his value and proclaims it by his actions. Remember, no one knows you better than you do yourself. If you tell an employer that you are ideal for his job and you will do it just fine, whether you are sure you can or not, then the other fellow does not have any better evidence of your abilities than what you tell him.

I remember my first week at grammar school. The sports master addressed all of us first year students.

'Who wants to be captain of the football team?' he asked. A dozen hands shot up. The sports master chose my friend Harold, whose hand was highest, thrust upwards with force. He really wanted it.

Meanwhile, the rest of us held our hands at half-staff for fear of seeming pushy or immodest. A great lesson I never forgot. It is still with me as I write this, just on sixty years later. Never be afraid to push yourself forward.

Part of the problem is that many students, especially those who did not go to the sort of school where students are trained for success, lack the basic self-confidence needed to grab the winner's trophies. If you have attended an ordinary school, you will have had little experience of meeting the rich and successful and learning how to be like them..

Never be afraid to push yourself forward !

It is difficult to feel much personal self-confidence if all the lessons from early life have put a limit on how far you can go in your career. If you are from a poor home much of your unconscious early training will have been learning, not how to be a success, but how to cope with failure or mediocrity.

I am not disparaging such training. If no-one you have ever known has ever made much of their career, then real success will not be something they can tell you about from personal experience.

Undoubtedly, the best way to become successful yourself is to grow up surrounded by successful people. These are the real teachers from whom you will learn, not just the names of useful contacts, but the internalized message that becoming successful is what is going to happen to you.

In my own experience, the very rich and successful are not always brighter or even more industrious than the journeyman plodder. The defining difference is their self-image as someone who deserves success. They have been told enough times during their early life that success is their due, their birthright.

One of the most important things a new graduate must do is to develop this mindset in him/herself. You must believe that you have the right, as much as or more than anyone else, to success and all its benefits. If you can do that, then all the necessary things you need to do to realize your ambitions will be so much easier.

Remember that this is a one-shot life, so you should not be bound by the limitations of the previous generation. You must make a conscious effort to redefine your self-view from loser to winner. That is easier said than done, of course. It requires a conscious mental effort and attention to all sorts of details. about how you run your life, from self-presentation to careful attenttion to the workplace politics, from personal financial management to careful career planning.

Going to graduate school

It is a myth that getting a graduate degree. e.g. an MBA, will put you ahead of the crowd in the race for the best jobs. Further study will be expensive so making a substantial addition to your student loan has to be very carefully considered.

This consideration explains why there has been a trend lately for high school leavers to miss out on college all together and go straight into a job or apprenticeship where they can start earning immediately without the burden of a large college debt.

Some employers will pay the whole or part of the tuition costs for an MBA course done part-time or online but for the person funding themselves, the investment may just not be worth it. You may think that a master's degree will get you a larger salary but the differences may not be all that large and your graduate study may never pay for itself.

You should also consider the time and energy which getting a graduate degree takes. They might be better spent elsewhere, for example, on your main job.

Another consideration is that if you study for your

master's immediately after taking your bachelor's then when you graduate, you will be competing in the job market with younger applicants.

A graduate degree may also put off an employer who employs new graduates. He may well believe that an MBA applying for a job which needs only a BS will see it as second best, having failed to get their first choice.

Whether you should go to graduate school depends a lot on the field you intend to go into. For example, if you want to be a college professor or physician, then a doctorate is mandatory. And if are going to work in an organization which employs large numbers of MBA's, you will be well-advised to get one yourself. In other places, fast track promotion may require the master's and not having it may impede your progress.

If you are going to be doing graduate study part-time it is probably a good idea to put it off until the moment is right. Your career may diverge in the meantime.

When choosing a graduate school to enrol at, beware the many substandard degree mills which offer an MBA after just a few months of online study. There can be few schools, however dubious, which have not plugged themselves into the lucrative online MBA market. Fees these places may be high but graduation is guaranteed and the workload is not too heavy.

Be sure instead to choose a well-known school with a reputation. There are enough of them around that a well-qualified graduate can be sure of getting a place in one of them. When people ask where you did your graduate study, you do not want to be humiliated when they ask '.. ..the university of *where*...?!?'

4 Networking

Building your own network

Networking has to start in college and has to be enthusiastically kept up throughout your career. Why are there so many clubs, organizations, associations, societies, if not to provide a way for one person to meet another?

We trade on our contacts all the time. If you do a job for a guy and he likes it, you have made a contact and he will come back a second time for more work because we go back to people whose work we can trust. There might be better people out there but who cares, if we can put work the way of a friend who will do what we need for a fair price?

Name recognition is the first aim. How can you make your way in the world if no one knows your name? A good way of making your name known is to join things. You must certainly join your professional society. If you are a new graduate then, whatever your discipline, there will be a learned society of people in the same profession – surveyors, economists, biologists, engineers – there is an association or society for every profession or interest under the sun.

What is more, the top names in your field will also be members of the same society. Go to the meetings, get known and pretty soon you will be on nodding terms with the stars of your chosen profession.

You could offer to give a presentation at one of the meetings to enhance your profile. Or you could do some of the behind-the-scenes menial work such as preparing the refreshments or operating the slide projector. What you need to be is to be seen to be an 'insider' – someone who is always around. Make yourself indispensable and the people whose ear you need will soon get to know who you are.

Stay in contact with your old college via the alumni association. It won't take up much time or money but it will keep you in touch, not so much with your old drinking buddies, but with that guy from your old class that you never really liked but who is now running for the Senate. Remember that he needs friends and supporters as well. When he gets into the Senate he is going to need people around him whom he can trust because we 'go way back'.

Going to conferences

Conferences are very good places for networking. Make sure that you go to at least one a year. Strangely, a lot of people do not like conferences and, it is true, some conferences can be deadly boring if you are only there to listen to the speeches and read the posters.

But conferences are not about the speeches and the handouts, they are about the off-stage networking. Everyone is doing it. That is what conferences are really for, the opportunity to meet other people who are also networking.

Take plenty of calling cards and have a few CV's on hand in case you get a bite. Remember, a conference, even the social part of a conference, is not about pleasure, it is about work. So be sure to look good and stay sober.

Do not worry about being too obvious when you are canvassing potentially useful people. They are doing it themselves and they expect professional newcomers to flatter them. They will be cultivating bigger fish than they are. In turn, they expect to be getting strokes from those, like you, who are even further down the food chain.

When it comes to building a large contacts database, always remember the blue skies rule – when chatting someone up, it is best if you concentrate on what you can do for them rather than what they can do for you.

So the great man needs some photocopying of his conference speech, does he? Yes, you will do it gladly.

What, the congressman suddenly needs to send an urgent email? Then please, sir, use my laptop.

These little acts of courtesy and kindness generate gratitude out of all proportion to the slight inconvenience it causes you. And if you can get one of these VIP's in conversation, always be ready, if they should mention a problem, with the ever-valuable phrase, 'How can I help you?'

Other things to join

Depending on your line of work, there are Rotary Clubs, Masonic Lodges and Chambers of Commerce to be joined. These will provide contacts with small local businesses. They are probably not too helpful if you are trying to make your way as a nuclear scientist but who knows, they are always on the lookout for speakers who can talk for half an hour about some unusual topic.

And even if you are a nuclear scientist, it is always useful to have a second string to your reactor as a resource speaker. Besides, these local organizations are full of useful people like builders and plumbers. Even nuclear scientists need builders and plumbers from time to time.

Local political parties are also useful. In the UK, the Conservative Party is always looking for new blood. Its members are usually older and richer than your average citizen. You may, or may not, agree with their politics, it doesn't matter. In the rat race, there is no place for political principles. In the US, you can become a registered Democrat or Republican, it matters little which, since the main object is to make useful contacts, getting seen and known.

There are local community groups, parent-teacher associations, charity groups, churches, evening classes and many others. There are potentially useful contacts in all of them.

Using social media

These days there are numerous social media where you are supposed to make useful contacts. *Facebook* is the most famous. I am a bit wary of *Facebook* – it seems to be too full of social chit-chat and everyday trivia. I wonder if *Facebook* is a non-sexual version of those dating sites where people embellish the truth about themselves.

'*Here I am in the Library of Congress where I am researching the decline of deponent verb usage in late Anglo-Saxon*' certainly sounds classier than '*I like to get rotten drunk every Friday night.*'

Anyone who has ever used a dating site knows that '*thirty-something, sexy, love machine with GSOH*' may be a little way off the truth. They may instead be a hard-bitten humourless sixty-year old.

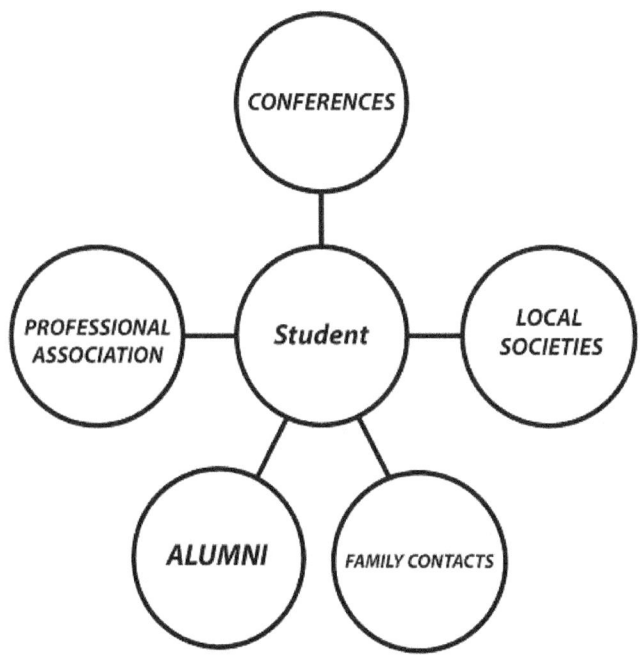

All the world's a network !

I am also a little apprehensive about telling the world about my personal life. *Facebook* makes me feel exposed. As for *Twitter*, I have yet to work out what is the point of it. I occasionally get spam from *Twitter* inviting me to 'follow' some well-known person like Lady Gaga or Bruce Willis or even someone I've never heard of. Why ever would I want to do that, I always wonder when they 'tweet' me?

I do use *LinkedIn*, which is supposed to be for professionals. In my experience it works OK. I have made a few useful contacts through it although I think its benefits are a little overblown. My connections tend to be old students who see me on *Linkedin* and remember that I can write them a glowing testimonial. Which I am very happy to do, if they tell me what they want me to say.

In fact I answer all my emails, whoever they are from. As well as it being good manners to reply to someone who has taken the trouble to get in touch with you, it keeps the relationship open.

These days, manners no longer makyth man, it seems. It now appears to be OK not to reply to emails because your time is too valuable. You must always reply to every communication. I can't emphasize too much the importance of good manners when it comes to dealing with people.

If you are polite, obliging and friendly, others will like you. If you don't reply to their messages, they won't send you anymore. What could be more obvious? The moral is – answer them all.

Handling rejection

When it comes to networking, we have all had to cope with rejections from time to time. It is part of the human condition. But even rejection need not be permanent. Let me give you a simple example.

Suppose you are setting up in business as, say, a landscape gardener. You will try to network all the property developers in your area.

Now, since you are new, your first trawl for business will be unsuccessful because these guys will already have their own landscapers. But the exercise is not wasted for two reasons.

First, it is quite possible that they will, from time to time, be let down by their preferred landscaper for many possible reasons. For example he may be double-booked. The property developer is then in a fix. If you have kept your name and phone number in front of him, he may well come to you to get him out of a spot.

The second reason is that property developers know other property developers whom you don't know and your name could be passed on. It is important always to keep your name in front of potential clients. It is bread on the water.

Advertising yourself

Had you ever wondered why large companies spend vast amounts of money on advertising their products? Well, to sell them, of course. But, if you see an advert for, let us say, the latest BMW car, are you tempted to rush out and buy it straight away? No, you are not and neither is anybone else. So why do BMW do it if it doesn't result in an immediate uptake in sales?

The answer is that advertising works by repetition. The commercials keep the BMW name in front of their intended clientele and, as far as possible, the placing of the adverts is where potential BMW buyers will be found. They present the company image – upmarket, classy, efficient, expensive - to continually reassure their clientele that they have made the right choice. Advertising, even without fast results, obviously works. It is a very large industry.

That is how you should approach the advertising of your own personal brand i.e. yourself. Think of yourself as a product you are marketing. This means monitoring the feedback you get at interviews and in your network and modifying your résumé, and the positions you apply for, accordingly. And not just your résumé. Your calling cards, carrying your name, specialism and contact details, should be regularly updated. .

You might also consider setting up your own website. It is not expensive. If you don't have programming skills yourself, then ask a friendly geek to do it for you. Add a 'counter' to your website so that you can monitor the traffic going to it - there are many free counters listed on *Google*.

Always be sure to follow up any interest shown in employing you, however flaky the contact might look at first sight. It just might be that call from the one person who is going to change your life forever.

5 The job interview

The four P's

A job interview is a business meeting. Your interviewer is investing time and effort in meeting you and there is a formal etiquette to be observed, one of good manners and mutual respect. The interview is an important step in the process of getting a job.

If you get to the interview stage it means that you are down to the last half dozen or fewer, since no company wants to spend a lot of time and money on interviewer time or interviewee expenses unless they are serious. How do you succeed at an interview? Important is to remember the four 'P's' - Preparation, Punctuality, Presentation and Personality.

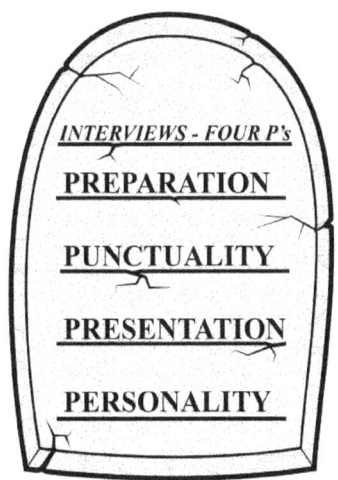

The four vital P's for interview success

Preparation

You must never go into a business meeting unprepared. If he goes on to hire you, the interviewer will be looking at your skills in preparing for future business meetings. He is looking at how you handle yourself.

So do your homework. Thoroughly research the company. Check out its financials, business issues and its competitors using sites like *Yahoo! Google*, and *Wikipedia*. Take time to carefully review the job description or advertisement so that you are absolutely sure you know exactly what the company is looking for.

Put as much work into the preparation as you would put into your final graduation term paper – hours, days even, until you know everything about the other side of the interview desk as you possibly can and make sure all that knowledge is instantly at your fingertips. You want that dream job, so work for it !

Prepare short mental narratives of how and when you have done each thing that might be mentioned. Be prepared to talk about obstacles you encountered and how you dealt with them successfully. And, by all means, be prepared to talk about past achievements that you have attained which in any way relate to the job vacancy.

Punctuality

Punctuality is vital. If you are late for an important interview, then the interviewer will deduce that you are likely to make an unpunctual employee. What is more, unpunctual often equates to being unreliable in other, or all, areas of professional behavior.

Why is punctuality so very important? Well, let me give you an example. Suppose you were to submit a very expensive long drawn out project proposal. The client will have taken competing bids, which for legal reasons will need to be submitted by a certain time, let us say 10.00 am on a specific day. At ten o'clock, precisely to the second, the client will be legally bound to refuse further bids. If you were just one second late, all the expensive work on the bid will have been wasted.

In exactly the same way, if you are late for your interview the interviewer may refuse to see you at all, so all that preparation will also have been wasted.

On the day of the interview, you should arrive very early, perhaps an hour before the specified time. If you plan for an hour ahead, you will not be flustered if you are delayed by traffic or you get lost.

Don't drive yourself to an interview because you may find yourself parking a mile away in the rain. Take a taxi.

Sit outside the building for most of the spare hour if you can. Use the time to watch the comings and goings of the people who might be your future co-workers. Observe – do they look harassed or stressed? Are they rushing around or are they relaxed?

Do not turn up at the actual interview itself more than five minutes ahead of schedule. (Do not, of course, be late!) Make sure you have done the last minute grooming - you should take with you a comb, a toothbrush and some tissues.

Presentation

Presentation says much about a candidate. You must always look your best. You might think it is superficial to judge a person by their external appearance but that is what everyone does and first impressions count most.

Men should be well-shaved and clean, with hair well cut, and shoes polished. This interview may turn out to be a turning point in your life so don't blow it for want of attention to detail. Wash and dry your hands before going in so you don't have sweaty palms for the introductory handshakes. Do not eat anything strong before the interview so that your breath smells sweet.

Presentation winner or loser? Which are you?

Make sure you have a notebook and a pen to note down any important information you might be given.

You should have a pristine, flat, not folded, copy of your résumé / CV for the chair of the meeting.

If you are asked to wait, then do not sit down, even if invited. Everyone looks better standing and you will create a more favourable first impression. This applies even if you are asked to wait in an empty room.

Make sure your cellphone and your other electronic devices are turned off. When the interview starts, let the interviewer sit first.

Naturally, you should be turned out in formal office attire – a suit for men and a business suit or a formal dress for women. (See Chapter 11)

Personality

Finally, personality and the interview itself. Do not appear humble, overly modest or unduly respectful. The interviewer is seeking some spark in you which sets you apart from the other hopefuls.

Do not, of course, overdo it and be too brash. Fluent, relaxed and confident is what the interviewer wants to see. These are important business personal skills and the interviewer wants to hire them. Someone who has these skills is more likely to succeed in future meetings with the company's clients.

Business negotiations require two players, just like the tango. The interviewer does not want to have to drag information out of you. He/she wants you to volunteer your side as well by giving full anwers to his questsions.

You are negotiating for your best advantage and both of you want to strike the best deal. Remember, they want to buy your talents at their lowest price and you want to get them to buy those talents and to pay your best price for them. Simple, isn't it?

If you don't know the answer to a question, say so, don't waffle. There is no shame in not knowing everything. After the formalities, the 'good mornings' and the introductions, your first words should be something like, 'Thank you for inviting me, I really appreciate it.' Good manners always !

You may have been told to send a follow-up email after the interview. No, this advice is wrong. A follow-up email comes across as ingratiating and desperate. The interviewer may even resent your wasting his time.

Ten interview questions they always ask

Apart from the technical questions which you will be asked to make sure that you know your subject, you can be absolutely certain that your interviewers will ask you some or all of the following ten questions. They are standard text-book interview questions. You should have ready-made answers to them.

1 What do you know about this company?

You should thoroughly have researched the company on the Internet and in the financial press. You should have a brief summary of the company, size, structure and the products it makes at your finger tips.

A knowledge of its financial position will show that you understand the nature of business. Knowing the history of the company is also helpful, especially if the company is long established or famous.

Find out, if you can, what kind of people the company likes to hire and how closely you meet their standards.

Be prepared with mental scripts in which you mention these points where you have things in common. Maybe 'when I was at Stanford ...' if you know that several people in the department also studied there.

2. Why do you want to leave your present company?

This applies only to changing jobs, but if you are asked about your present company, be complimentary about it. If the new company is in the same line of business as the company you are with now, and especially if they are in the same city, your interviewers may well be personal friends of your present bosses.

You are moving on because you are seeking new opportunities to advance yourself. You are ambitious and you want to get on. You see the new company as a place where you can expand your talents and your horizons.

Never, never, never bad-mouth your present employer even if he makes Attila the Hun look like Saint Theresa. Bad-mouthing makes you look untrustworthy. If you are moving between companies in the same industrial sector, your interviewer will know all about the problems in your present company.

3. Why do you want to work here?

From what you have read, this company is expanding into new products and markets and it has a lot of future potential. It would be good to be part of that. It is a promising industry sector you are keen to get into.

4. How much salary do you expect to earn?

You expect to be paid whatever is their norm. You intend to show by results that you will be able to earn regular salary increases as you demonstrate your usefulness to the company.

5. Where do you expect to be in 6 months/1 year/5 years?

You are confident that you will earn promotion over time as you show that you are able to take on more responsibility. An attractive candidate is one who comes across as confident in their abilities without being too 'pushy'.

6. What are your long term ambitions?

Here you can try a small joke such as '*well, who can predict the future..*' or '*it would be nice to be rich and famous, but..*'. Tell them that your long-term ambitions are to secure a place in senior, strategic management where you can have a major say in the future development of this industry.

If they follow up with a question like how you see the long–term strategic developments, you will have done your reading.

By the way, use humour sparingly. One small joke is enough to show that you do have a sense of humour but do not overdo it. They do not want to hire a comedian.

7. What are your strengths?

Here the interviewers are waiting to hear things like good academic record, personal initiatives which show that you are a self-starter, that you are good at working with others, that you are a team player and you have good analytic and creative skills.

If you have good communication skills in written English, then be sure to mention this. New graduates who are deficient in writing abilities, especially report writing, are the despair of many employers. Your résumé will have given a clear indication of how well or badly you write.

If you have done some serious out-of-school voluntary work, mention it. It will go down well.

8. Do you have any weaknesses?

Of course you have weaknesses. Everybody has weaknesses. When you are asked this common question, do not tell the interviewer that your weakness is that you are too hard-working or that you always rise to a challenge. He will not believe you.

He is looking for someone to do a specific job. The purpose of this question is so that he can find out what you lack when it comes to fitting the person to the vacant situation..

You should have read the job description carefully and you should know what parts of it you are weak in. That's what he is trying to find out. If there are parts of the job description you do not feel confident about, then come clean. The interviewer will appreciate your not wasting his time.

9. How can we use you best?

You may think your particular strengths are in, maybe, analytical work and computer model building, or whatever. Obviously the precise answer depends on the nature of the company. The interviewers are looking for a good fit in their own workforce.

Try to give an impression of adaptability without being too open-brained about it. You can say that you are keen to widen your experience to apply your present skills to new problems.

10. Do you want to ask us a question?

Always ask one or two intelligent questions to show that you are a serious contender. If the interview has been a proper two-way dialogue, you will already have the answers to the important questions so this final courtesy is no more than that. But it is bad manners not to have anything to ask.

Demonstrate your seriousness by asking, for example, 'How does this company do its performance evaluations?' or 'What is your reporting line?'

Or maybe you could ask 'What are the most important contributions I could make in the first year on the job?'

Bad questions to ask are 'How many weeks holiday will I get?' and 'Am I expected to work overtime?'

The interview is a two-way process

You, the interviewee, need not be not passive or defensive. You are not on trial. You are also measuring up the company for how well it suits your own longer term ambitions. After all, you are likely to be spending a good proportion of your life there.

So you also want to find out for yourself whether the job, if you are offered it, is really what you want. This is a big step – you do not want to grab the first job you are offered if it is wrong for you just because you are afraid you might not get another offer.

It is important that you get as accurate a picture as possible by your own personal observations. The formal information about a company which appears in the press/websites etc. is not going to be complete.

You should look out for answers to seven basic questions which you should ask yourself in order to decide whether the job is for you, according to Dr Marla Gottschalk, a famous industrial psychologist.

Dr Marla's questions are:

1 *Does the role align with my strengths?*
2 *How will I be spending my day?*
3 *Does the role have a future?*
4 *Am I like the other individuals that have succeeded in this organization?*
5. *What challenges is the organization facing?*
6 *What metrics will be utilized to measure my performance?*
7 *Where do I stand?**

---

*Dr Marla Gottschalk'*7 Questions You Must Absolutely Answer in a Job Interview'*. Pub. Linkedin on September 16th 2013

Keeping your eyes and ears open when you are on the company premises is very important. A friend of mine was a natural businessman who was used to dealing with lots of different types of companies. He always mistrusted companies with glossy frontages.

Companies making money do not waste it on unnecessary ostentation. He was particularly mistrustful of companies which had a fountain in the lobby and receptionists adorned in expensive designer uniforms.

Here is something I have noticed when I have been interviewed by relatively junior staff and that is that they will sometimes unconsciously give away snippets of personal information which reveal something about the company. They won't say, of course, that this is a terrible company and you shouldn't bother with trying to get a job here but, being relatively unpromoted themselves, they might, occasionally, make some oblique reference to their frustration.

For example, I once went for an interview for a job with a top American chemical company. We met in the interviewer's shabby, cubby-hole office which he shared with his secretary. 'I've been here for twenty nine years,' he told me.

The man did not realize how much information he was giving away by that seemingly neutral remark. He was telling me that he had been shunted into a dead end and that his career had gone nowhere. After twenty nine years, he was still only interviewing the graduate intake ! Be on the lookout for this kind of incidental useful information unconsciously dressed up as innocent comment. Remember always that an interview is a two-way street – both sides of the table are there to gather information about the other before the final deal is concluded.

The four basic interviewer styles

Interviewers each have their individual ways of interviewing but four basic styles can be identified. Most interviewers have a single preferred style.

1 The simple question and answer

> The first type is a *viva voce* exam, where the interviewer asks the questions after the manner of a professor quizzing a master's degree graduate student. Simple factual answers are all that is required. The interviewer will not be interested in whether your face will fit in the workplace, only whether you have been honest on your CV or application form and to discover any supplementary information the company might need.
>
> This type of interview is often the preliminary interview in a multi-level selection process. The interviewer who uses this technique will not have a very high rank in the company. His job is simply to elicit the facts about you and report them back.
>
> Later interviews will be held with increasingly senior people who will be less concerned with what you know and more about whatever personal and social qualities you might possess.

2. The cross-examination

Another interview technique is the quasi-forensic cross-examination. The style is used by interviewers who have watched too many gritty court room movies. Think of Tom Cruise in *'A Few Good Men'* or Gregory Peck in *'To Kill a Mockingbird'*. The interviewer, who fancies himself (or herself, the style is not sexist) as a tough, sharp, brilliant cookie, if you don't mind, will probe the candidate for weaknesses in their application. Expect questions like

'You claim to have experience of retailing, Mister... but you were only with Bigga Stores for two years. Would you say that entitles you to say you have much experience of retailing?'

Or they might ask,

'You say you left InterMart after only two years and four months, but that's not true is it? Isn't it the case that you only spent nineteen months as a full-time employee – the other five months, no, nearly six months, you were only an intern?'

One type of question this type of interviewer likes to throw at you is the 'loyalty' question. (See Chapter 10 for more on the loyalty question.)

'So you left Bigga Stores after only two years.

That doesn't show much loyalty to them, does it?'

To all these questions, answer levelly and try not to get rattled. That is what he may be trying to do, unsettle you. If you want the job well enough, then you can give them straight answers and hope for the best. If the questions get too intrusive or rude, you can always get up and go.

3. The fireside chat

At the other end of the scale from the cross-examination is the discursive chat. The interview appears formless, directionless, as the interviewer draws you out in a seemingly random conversation. You could easily find yourself in very deep water indeed. It is only human that we respond to friendliness by sharing personal information in return. If you don't keep your guard up, you could find yourself disclosing things about yourself which would be better left hidden.

Be aware, be very aware, because this interviewer is not your friend. The whole point of an interview of this type is to make you give away things you have deliberately left off the résumé. Application forms and résumés are never just about the plain unvarnished truth. They are about what we would prefer the plain unvarnished truth to have been.

If the Perry Mason type of interviewer is a rottweiler, then this Mister Nice Guy is a friendly boa constrictor.

4. The 'let's do a deal' interview

By far the best type of interview is the straightforward, cards-on-the-table, no-nonsense business negotiation. The interviewer doesn't want to waste any time. He just wants the best deal at the best price as quickly as possible. If your interviewer is this type, then count yourself lucky.

A good interview is a negotiation towards a deal based on a natural rapport between the interviewer and interviewee.

Successful interviews are those where there is a natural rapport between interviewer and interviewee. Questions are asked and answered at a normal conversational rate. Points are taken up in their proper sequence, each one segueing into the next fluently.

Always remember that the interviewer is investing a lot of time and money in this interview. His/her aim is to get the best deal for the company. A good interviewer will negotiate towards that deal. As the interviewee, your role is to help him reach his decision, hopefully by choosing you.

Interview by a panel or committee

In the public sector, hiring and firing is always a committee decision, unlike in private companies, where decisions may be entrusted to individuals. For a town hall- or an academic job interview, a panel, sometimes called a search committee, will be set up. If you are faced with a panel, there will be a mixture of the four basic interview styles.

The chair of the panel need not be the most important member. He/she may just be a neutral figurehead, brought in to give the interview process a patina of fairness, especially if the real winner has already been chosen. (There is no evidence that 'jobs for the boys' does not apply in public sector appointments and there is plenty of evidence that it does.)

The use of a supposedly neutral chairman by an interview panel is the sort of thing which can be put in the reply to the letter of complaint when the obviously best candidate writes to his elected representative that the job went instead to the well-connected village idiot.

Faced with an interview panel with many different interviewer types, one must be very quick at moving from one mode of answer to another. You must be able to change your personality swiftly, from aggressive to friendly decent fellow as the response requires.

Panels are also a way to intimidate a candidate by numbers. Do not be intimidated. Remember, you can always walk out if you don't like the way it is going. If you do walk, make sure that it is in response to a question from a person you do not like. Take personal offence at what the fellow said, then get up, thank the chairman and walk out. It won't do you any good, but the fellow who asked the question might just get into hot water later because he was the cause of a waste of time.

If you are faced by a panel, then at least the employer is serious. An appointment will be made and it could be you, unless they already know who they want. Panels will meet several candidates on the same day so the later you are called before them, the lower your chances of getting the job because of simple math.

Let us suppose that there are six of you up for the job and each is interviewed by a panel, then it follows that, even if you all start level with a 1/6 chance of winning, the last guy in will still have a 1/6 chance although it is now a 5/6 chance that the panel has already chosen one of the others.

Panels get tired after a few hours of asking the same questions to the six hopefuls so they may decide early on to give the job to someone who is good enough.

If your interview is late in the day and the panel look fed up and uninterested, their body language may make it clear that they have already come to their verdict and they have already chosen another candidate. However, since you have traveled overnight from the other side of the country, they will feel that they have to go through the motions and pretend that you are still in with a chance. If that happens to you, then you can just go home, or you can try to squeeze a little amusement out of the situation by playing the interview for the laughs.

Sometimes the chairman of the panel may be the same perosn who will become your boss. If the chair of the panel is a neutral, then the most important panel member will usually be found sitting next to them.. Rank tends to decline with the distance from the centre. There is no formal rule about this, but that's how it usually works out.

After a few minutes you should be able to pick out which of the panel are important and who are only there to make up the numbers.

Obviously, you should direct your important answers and eye contact at those important few. The others, the 'padding' of the panel, will only ask the odd, unimportant question. If they take up too much time, they will quickly be slapped down by the chair.

Look out for the type of interview where there is a silent panel member taking notes. This happened to me once when I was in for a job at a college in South Wales. The interview went along standard lines until the very last question.

The chairman then turned to the large quiet man who had said nothing throughout.

'Anything?' he asked.

The man shook his head and I got the job. I found out later that he was the local political fixer whose duty it was to approve all job applicants for political reliability in what was a one-party town.

Sometimes, not getting the job is your best move. I remember one interview I went to in Aberdeen, a two-day affair involving an eight-hour drive each way. It was midsummer, so the heat was at its peak, which, in northern Scotland means 15C. I was also told that midwinter could see as little as four hours of daylight.

I looked around the grey granite desolation and decided that no way did I want to come here. But, I had been warned, if I had been offered the job and I had turned it down, they would not pay my considerable interview expenses.

A good bit of advice. When my turn came to present myself to a twenty-strong committee of dour Scottish interviewers I had to work hard to make sure I came across as a thoroughly useless candidate.

Ten mistakes interviewees make

1 Being late

Unpunctuality is an absolute deal-breaker in a job interview. If you are late for no reason, the interviewer will conclude that you are a person completely devoid of all moral character.

2. Forgetting that first impressions count most

We judge people on first impressions. Within a very short time of meeting a new person we decide in our minds whether the other person is honest, sly, trustworthy, reliable, weak or strong, likeable or repulsive. We use a million instinctive clues to sum up the newcomer within 30 seconds.

A job interview is not just the formal questioning. It begins the moment you enter the building and lasts until you finally depart the premises.

What is more, you must stay alert for the whole time you are in the building. A single lapse in your manner or your appearance will be noticed by someone and reported on.

Everyone who sees you or talks to you while you are at the company's premises will form an opinion of you. Even people who are not involved in recruitment process, such as the guard on the front desk or the woman who serves the coffee, may well be asked what they thought about you.

3. Not presenting yourself properly

Bad grooming, or attending the interview dressed casually, e.g. in blue jeans and sneakers, will definitely damage your chances of interview success. The interview is a formal occasion, so you must dress accordingly. (See Chapter 11)

4. Appearing distracted or uninterested.

You appear distracted or bored when you shift in your chair or cross/uncross your legs. Demonstrate interest by leaning slightly forward, lifting your head, and nodding on occasion.

5. Bad posture.

Do not slouch in the interview chair. Sit up straight and lean forward slightly. This will show you to be confident and alert.

If your head leans to one side when you speak, you are unconsciously giving off a body-language message that you are not telling the truth.

6. Too weak or too strong a handshake.

A weak handshake is a subconscious sign that you do not want proper contact with the other person. It is an unconscious signal of rejection.

On the other hand, if your handshake is hand-crushingly strong, you are giving out the signal that you are unconsciously trying too hard to be dominant.

7. Not making eye contact.

Make sure you offer the appropriate amount of eye contact, Failure to make eye contact looks shifty and dishonest.

8. Not being prepared with examples that illustrate why you'd excel at the job

Even if everything you need to know has been covered in the interview, you should still find some questions to ask. It shows you are serious.

9 Not smiling

Smile and the world smiles with you. It is important that you project a positive out-going personality. No one wants to work with colleagues who are miserable or self-obsessed.

10. Not being likeable

Interviewers are human and they want to work with pleasant people. The interviewer will, in all probability, make his final decision on 'gut instinct' i.e. whether he likes you or not.

Sometimes the company may give you a post-interview de-briefing. It can be very useful, not for what it says, but what it leaves out.

They may use vague phrases like *'we didn't feel that you would quite fit into our setup'* or *'the panel felt that you are over-qualified for the job'*.

Both answers mean that you could do the job well enough but that they just did not like you. Do not let this upset you: you may have escaped a job where you were required to work with people whom you would find equally incompatible.

6 Office politics

The big mistake new graduates make

When you get into a new job, you may be tempted to think that your new place is politics-free. You will overhear office gossip about senior management and what they get up to which might lead you to think that political machinations only take place at an elevated level.

Nothing is further from the truth. Politics involving you, yourself, begin the moment they make you a job offer. You will be sized up critically by your colleagues from the very start. Information about you may already be common knowledge among your new colleagues even before you start work on the first day.

Each of your co-workers will have their own personal agenda. You may even have a walk-on part in those agendas. The only thing which you can be absolutely sure of is that your own welfare and position is of absolutely no interest to them at all, however friendly they may seem.

The most serious big mistake which new employees make is to confuse the professional friendliness of their new workmates with genuine warmth. These people are not your friends. They are your co-workers, your colleagues, your competitors. When promotions or other goodies are up for grabs, they may even become your enemies.

Office politics is 'must-learn'

They don't tell you how to handle office politics when you are in college even though the professors are probably playing office politics themselves. Most likely, they are playing them badly. University departments are infested with self-serving incompetent amateur politicians.

Your level of skill at office politics is one of the most important things which will shape your career. Just because your own office is placid and well-run, it doesn't mean that office politics are absent, or even dormant, because even the best-run organization has office politics. It is reputed, for example, that The College of Cardinals in the Vatican has its own office politics, and very bitter they are said to be too.

Politics are everywhere. Recognising the presence of office politics and learning how to cope with them are essential arts which must, definitely must, be mastered quickly. Neglecting them may well turn you into one of those sad creatures who wonders why, in spite of his top class degree, his non-stop hard work and his long experience he always finds the promotions going to someone else.

Even though every organization has its office politics, it is possible to work with them, just as long as they are controlled and they don't disrupt the workday routine. But sometimes they can take over a large office or even an entire organization. When that happens, the whole working environment can become poisoned.

Bad office politics

An office will function badly if the office politics have been allowed to get out of control. An unhappy office environment is often down to one or two malevolent people and their cliques. Unchecked, those people can wreak havoc on the efficiency and morale of a workforce.

So, how do you spot when the office is in the grip of one of these people and their groupies? There are some obvious clues which the newcomer should be able to pick up right away.

For example, some workers will spend a lot of time gossiping about their co-workers. This will lead to an unspoken atmosphere of distrust.

In more serious cases, where the working environment has been seriously contaminated, there may be public arguments, regular complaints to higher authority, backstabbing, manipulating, controlling, finger pointing, power grabbing, idea stealing or credit taking.

If the newcomer finds him/herself thrown into such a bear pit, they will, in all probability, get taken on one side by a 'friendly' confidant and warned about the goings on.

You, the newbie, must be careful. The person confiding in you will certainly have an axe to grind. They may even be the root cause of the problem. Unasked-for confidences early in one's job could well be a move by a player who is looking for allies.

If there is more than one approach, each with revelations and warnings about someone else, then you can be sure that the workers are split into two or more factions whose origins lie in personal animosity.

If the primary cause of the atmosphere is down to a single individual, then the symptoms will disappear once the cause of the bad smell is removed.

But sometimes, that person will be the boss, or the manager of the office, which causes problems for everyone. But they could just as likely be a single malicious employee with unresolved personal issues.

If the root cause of the problems is he boss himself, then, if he is strong, then he will unite the workforce in opposition to him. Or he may be a weakling, in which case a stronger personality, nominally his subordinate, but with their own agenda, will have freedom to manipulate the rest of the staff.

You have a choice about how far you want to get involved with the infighting. It depends on how long you intend to stay in the job. You may just be passing through. For example, it may be a temporary job for you or it may be an internship or a starter job from which you are intending to move on at the first opportunity.

My advice then would be to stay out of the situation and refuse to join in the politicking. Maintain a cool distance. If you are indeed intending to move on and the boss is the cause of the trouble, then staying neutral may not help your testimonial letter. It is better to risk being damned with faint praise in a lukewarm reference than to make the wrong guess about the politics and get fired.

On the other hand, you may be a natural politician yourself. You may be one of those individuals who compensates for a lack of genuine talent by a shrewd understanding of human psychology and how it can be exploited..

You may even thrive in a combative and disputatious setup. Such talents have taken many second-raters a very long way in the past, even to the world's very top jobs.

The rules for surviving office politics

Whether you are a player or an avoider, there are two general principles which always apply.

First, always make sure that you leave personal relationships at the door. This is work, not a social club. Never confuse politeness and good manners with overtures of friendship.

Choose your friends from outside your workplace and be suspicious of any invitations to join in social activities with your colleagues. This is not always easy because you do not want to get a reputation for being unfriendly and stand-offish either. A few carefully-worded excuses will get the message across that you prefer to keep your work and your social life separate.

Second, you must always observe office standards when it comes to attendance, punctuality, dress and civility. Never give anyone a single excuse for criticism. If you are not aligned with a faction, then you will be an object of suspicion to both sides. One lapse in your standards will be enough to give the office gossips useful material for their spite.

If you have decided that you are not going to join in the politics because maybe, the job is just short-term, then there are twelve simple rules to see you through.

1 'To thine own self be true', as Shakespeare put it. Be yourself. Do not wear a false 'mask' to make an impression. Show people the real 'you', so that they cannot find false things to say about you behind your back.

2 Identify those people who might be the source of office political trouble. It is usually easy to work out who they are. Watch their behaviour – do they, for example, pass on gossip uninvited?
 Do not befriend them. Do not, for example, go to lunch or coffee with them. Ignore them if they seem to be interested in you.

3 Do not contribute to work-related gossip sessions. Walk away because staying there will make it seem like you approve of what they are saying. Gossip reflects on the gossiper, not the victim. If you gossip, it puts you in a bad light. When someone gossips to you, you should always ask yourself the following questions.

Why are they telling me this?
What is their motive for damaging the other person's reputation?
What are they going to say to me behind my back?

Remember at all times - VERBAL DISCIPLINE !

4 Keep your eyes and ears open. Know what is going on around you without joining in yourself. Often, a bad office situation is down to a single individual. It will become clear very quickly if that is the case.

The individual will either identify themselves or a gossiper will tell you who it is. What they tell you may be true or it may not. Do not repeat it. Simply file it away for possible future reference..

Indeed, treat all such informal information you come across as possibly untrue. It is a regrettable fact of life that people are not uniformly truthful. They tell lies.

Some lie because they have an ulterior motive in misleading you. Others lie to impress you. Yet others lie because they don't know how to make human conversation without lying. Always be sceptical of anything you hear. But there is no reason why you shouldn't overhear gossip. Just don't gossip yourself.

5 Always do what is right. Do not be drawn into doing something which you do not like or which you consider unethical.

6 Disclose the very minimum of personal information. Do not answer questions about your circumstances, such as - '*do you have children?*', '*do you have money worries?*', '*do you have problems at home?*', '*are you unhappy at not being promoted?*', '*are you*

thinking of applying for another job? Keep all this sort of information to yourself. It could eventually be used against you.

However hard you try to stay out of the fray, you will make enemies and your personal details will get passed on to people who could do you harm. No one ever keeps a secret.

If you are asked for some personal confidential information, always ask yourself how you would feel if the same confidential information were published world-wide on *Facebook*.

7 Never criticize ! Stay calm, no matter what the level of frustration. If someone has done you a bad turn, control your ego. An outburst will do you a lot of damage and you will be labeled a troublemaker.

You cannot avoid ever saying something about someone else unless you live the life of a Trappist recluse. But always be sure only to say good things about them. You may hate their guts but keep that to yourself.

Before you say something about someone else, think

> *Would I say this to their face?*
> *Will this exclude me from useful team projects?*
> *Do I really want to make an enemy of them?*
> *If she/he spoke about me like this, how hurtful would it be to me?*
> *What will their retaliation be?*

8 Always keep your boss informed about anything you think he/she should know. There is nothing a boss hates more than a surprise caused by someone who reports to him/her.

9 If you are doing something important, keep timed and dated records. If it is important enough, then get signatures of authorization. This is sometimes known as 'covering your backside'.

It is not unknown for a boss to give something risky to an expendable underling who can be blamed if it all goes wrong.

You have to work with your boss but in most lines of work, unless you are a presidential security guard, you are not expected to take a bullet for him. So always look after Number One.

10 Revenge is a dish best eaten cold, they say, so be patient. If someone has done you a bad turn, the best thing you can do is wait for them to fall on their face. Which they will if you wait long enough.

11 Focus on doing your job. That's why you come to the office, to do your job

12 Stay positive ! Smile and be friendly at all times.

These are simple rules which will protect you in a hostile environment, which many offices certainly are. The twelve rules work well enough if the job is temporary and if it is not what you really want to make your life's work.

Very occasionally, you may need to confront a bad situation head-on. People who play bad office politics to make their co-workers unhappy are usually insecure, unhappy people themselves. They always lack personal self-confidence. This means that a small set-back can cause them great self-doubt. Remember that the bully is often a coward. Sometimes a direct challenge will be enough to frighten them off.

Always turn your back on gossip.

Guarding against career sabotage

In many cases playing the office politics may be an unspoken part of your job. You may find yourself without the option of being an avoider. This happens when not playing and winning will result in serious career damage. If you are in this situation, it helps if you can identify your enemies. That may be a strong word to use about a co-worker, but remember, career success is not simply a game. It carries significant rewards for you and your family. Career failure comes with heavy penalties, personal and financial.

There are only so many prizes to be handed out. The other guys want them and they want you not to have them. So it is likely that, from time to time, you will meet a charming friendly face who wants to sabotage your career so they can take the goodies for themselves.

You may find yourself the object of a slanderous whispering campaign or bad reports to the boss. Many bosses will believe without question the stories which a malicious underling brings them about some other member of the department. Especially if the tales come from an employee whom the boss has made one of his favourites.

If you find yourself being conspired against like this, you may find your options are limited. If you complain to the boss, you may be accused of not being a team player and that could damage your future progress. On the other hand, if you sit back and do nothing, you might lose by default.

Sometimes it will be necessary to strike back or even to get your retaliation in first. The basic rule when you find yourself in an unwanted contest is not to hold back. If someone wants to sabotage your career, then they have earned the right to have their own career sabotaged in return. Await your chance. Make sure that you have a cast-iron case against them and a back-up plan if you don't win.

If a colleague is denigrating you or trying to steal the credit for your efforts, this is what you can do:

1 Make absolutely sure that he/she is the problem and that it is not you who is the one at fault.

2 Keep your cool and don't confront the saboteur.

3 If you are unsure of your position, consult a trusted mentor or senior colleague if you can find one.

4 If you still feel you are in the right, then talk to your boss about it. If the boss is weak, he may well be aware of the bad situation and be afraid to do anything. He may even dismiss your complaint and pass it on to your adversary. So be careful before you do this. It is almost the last resort.

5 If the boss is not prepared to back you but you still feel that you have a justifiable complaint against your opponent, then you can make a formal complaint to senior management. Your evidence will need to be fully documented and absolutely verifiable.

Be very, very careful before you take this final step. It is the final throw of the dice. Anyone who brings a formal grievance, even if you are proved to be right, is going to be remembered as a troublemaker. What is more, you will certainly have made an enemy of your line manager for going above his head. His boss, in turn, will see him as a man who cannot manage his department safely.

Even winning your grievance case may not be beneficial to your long term career. It may even be career-ending.

Inside your present company you will have cut yourself off from the promotion ladder forever. You may already be earmarked for dismissal or redundancy at the first opportunity.

Nor should you think that you can get another job in the same line of business. The grievance will be mentioned when your new intended employer calls your present company to ask why the formal testimonial letter was so lacking in detail and why it was so tepid about you.

The new company you want to move to will not take the risk of hiring someone who may have a taste for bringing formal grievances.

Rules for serious office politicians

If you are well into a career structure and you are getting reasonably skilled at the office politics game, then some further understanding of power and how it is achieved may be helpful.

If you are headed for senior management then you need to understand the power structure of your organization.

The first thing an aspiring senior executive must do is study the organization and its culture very carefully. There are five vital questions.

1 *Where does the real power lie?*

The formal management structure chart is usually an over-simplification of the real power structure in the business. There are always several overlapping hierarchies. A good example of this would be a hospital with three hierarchies which intermesh – the doctors, the nurses and the administrators, each of which will have a claim to the final word in medical decision-making.

Added to the multiple formal structures, most organizations also have power relationships between individuals and work groups which pay little heed to the formal levels of the participants as defined by the structure chart. Beneath the formal job descriptions lie all sorts of unspoken drives, obligations and ambitions.

Power is the ability to get things done or to stop them from getting done. The most powerful person in your company therefore may be someone quite inconspicuous. In many organizations that person might be the office manager, the president's personal assistant or even his secretary.

The real actual power in a company may lie not with senior executives but instead with a person who will have little formal executive authority themselves. Such a person can sanction or deny essential access to important people and they can facilitate or frustrate the day-to-day work of much better paid and higher-ranking executives. There is at least one such person in every organization. Become their friend !

She may be paid a lot less than you but she has a direct line to the CEO and you don't

2 *How are decisions made?*

Are decisions made by a board or a committee or by single individuals? If it is a committee, then who is on it? Why are they there? For example, it has been said that the most powerful man in the United States administration is not the President but the Chairman of the Senate Ways and Means Committee.

In your own organization, the most serious, important decisions may actually be made by an all-powerful committee with some neutral name such as *'The Planning and Review Standing Committee'* or *'The Interdepartmental Liaison Group'*.

If you work in a place which is ruled by such a committee, then obviously you should become friendly with as many members of it as you can, so that your name comes to mind the next time there is a vacancy on it.

3. *What are the core values of your organization?*

Organizations come to resemble each other in their management structures in the way that mammalian life forms - sheep or wolf or elephant *etc.* - are all built to the same basic pattern.

Organizations as diverse as Walmart, UNESCO or the Mafia have underlying similarities when it comes to the selection of individuals for promotion, the chains of command, reporting and so on.

It is vital that an ambitious and successful player

of office politics in any organization should absorb the corporate culture until it becomes a central feature of the personality they project at work. Big organizations will promote only on the basis of just how thoroughly the promotee has become indoctrinated into the ethos and attitudes of the organization – how far they have become 'one of us'

It is vital to believe the core message of the business, or at least to convince yourself, and everyone else, of course, that you truly, sincerely believe it! Hallelujah !

4 *Are short- or long-term results more important?*

Your organization's vision is short-term or long-term will be reflected in the stability of its workforce. Retailing and hospitality concerns tend to be short-term whereas large established multinationals or civil service departments are long term.

Smaller private outfits tend to be more short-term than larger ones. As a rule, short-term concerns will have a faster staff turnover and quicker promotions than long-term businesses. An office politician will be able to use this knowledge to advantage when planning the timing of his/her career steps.

The ambitious careerist can move more quickly up an organization which has a short term focus.

Building a career in a long-term outfit is often a matter of waiting for 'dead man's shoes'. It is a question of your personality which you prefer.

5 *How much risk is tolerated?*

When someone comes to me with an idea which is flawed, they sometimes say 'it's a calculated risk' to which I always reply, 'then show me the calculations'. There aren't any calculations. The word 'calculated' is merely inserted to give the false impression that a dubious or risky plan has been properly thought through.

People and companies may be natural risk-takers or naturally risk averse. This is not a constant because both can move from being risk-takers to risk-avoiders and *vice versa*. It is also oversimplifying things to say that young companies are risk-takers and older companies are risk-averse.

Sometimes a long-standing company may rethink its strategy with regard to risk if there is a change in the business environment. This is what happened in the 1990's when banking regulationsin the US and Europe were relaxed. The result was that long-established ultra-conservative low-risk retail banks morphed into high-risk investment houses.

You should be quite clear which kind your company is at the time. The ambitious executive who suggests a high-risk scheme to a risk-averse company is making a bad political move which will be interpreted by his more staid peers as a reckless lack of judgement.

On the other hand, someone who advocates caution and inaction to a risk-taking company may likewise be condemned as too careful and conservative for high office.

Risk-averse people will be unhappy in a risk-taking company. People who are comfortable with a high level of risk because of the rewards which risk can bring, will find themselves frustrated in a risk-averse set-up.

Why office politics are important

Students of office politics should learn from the old masters. Read, for example, how Napoleon and Julius Caesar got the top jobs in their organizations. Both exhibited ruthless single-mindedness.

Shakespeare's plays about the power politics which Caesar and Macbeth were playing resonate today because they are about archetypes – exaggerated depictions of eternal human motivations. At work, you are in a power struggle, literally for life. Do you not want food and comfort and the most attractive mate? Or, in modern terms, a bigger house, a smarter car and a posher school for your children?

You may not notice it but everyone around you is also playing the office politics game. Many people, probably most, are instinctively political without, often, consciously thinking about what they are doing. Take some time to analyze what is going on and raise your consciousness to understand the political motivations of your colleagues. Everyone has an angle.

Not playing the office politics

Since we are all caught up in office politics whether we like it or not, it makes sense to learn to play it well. Not to play it at all is a sure guarantee of failure. Non-players, especially those who disdain the game as beneath them, will definitely lose out.

Some people take the fastidious line that office politics is not the sort of thing a fair-minded human being should do. In an ideal world, that is a perfectly defensible position. But this is not an ideal world.

As we have said, politics is the art of understanding how to leverage a situation involving individuals to our advantage and, more importantly, to recognize when someone is doing the same thing to us. We can then apply the appropriate measures or counter-measures to ensure maximum return from what is, in reality, a simple zero-sum game - either I win and you lose or you win and I lose. But not everyone wants to play the game.

I have spent a working life of nearly sixty years surrounded by some very fine minds. I have known engineers, mathematicians, computer scientists and economists whose company I have been honoured to be in. Many were brilliant, with first class degrees and the sharpest, the most incisive of intellects.

One would have thought that these people, the cream of academia and certainly in the top micro-percent of human intelligence would have found themselves as leaders of their generation, their superior brains at the service of the whole of humanity.

But no, that is not what usually happened. Most of those fine minds did not rise to global, or even national, importance as gurus or leaders, as their abilities surely entitled them to. They reached a certain level, a level where their talents were only applauded by their peers. That was as far as it went.

These star brains broke one of the basic rules of the game. They made the mistake of thinking that they themselves were above the squalid street fighting of office politics. They considered themselves too superior for the dog fight. Surely academic brilliance is all it takes to demonstrate one's cleverness, isn't it?

At the same time, the worldlier, more streetwise, political animals recognized the latent potential in these characters but also their fatal flaws. The result was that the top jobs, those jobs with the most power and the highest salaries, would finish up in the hands of the second rate, those who had compensated for their intellectual ordinariness by enhancing their skills in manipulating interpersonal relationships.

Even if the worker is not brilliant, he may still be a solid worker who will never get promoted because he has been brought up to believe that it is bad form to sing his own praises or to play the politics game. He actually thinks, wrongly, that his talents will be recognized in due course. He has been too infected with the good manners of the decent fellow who believes that honest, hard-working people should always make sure their light is well hidden under a bushel. Sad to say, his modesty means that he may see out his entire career fruitlessly waiting for his talents to receive their due recognition.

The different types of office politician

Mister Showman

The first sort is what we might call the showman. He sings his own praises loudly but he never stays very long in any job before he moves on to something better paid. The showman will display an energetic creativity when discussing his long-term objectives but he will always move on before his ideas have to be tested operationally.

Instead, he will dump all the problems of his grand plans on to his successor. When it all goes pear-shaped, the showman may be one or two jobs further on. Whoever is left picking up the pieces from the failed initiative may not even know who caused the foul-up in the first place.

One trick he often uses when he gets into a new middle management position is to spend two years or so on some study or investigation.

At the end of the two years, the study may be complete and the report will be written but it will be too soon to implement an action plan for it.

By now, though, the showman will have had two years in an important position, which should be long enough for him to have got himself another promotion somewhere else where he can repeat the process all over again.

If your co-worker is a Mister Showman, don't worry. They are only passing through.

Mister Ambitious Young Man

What Mister Ambitious Young Man lacks in experience, he makes up for in enthusiasm and aggression. Actually the AYM does not understand the game properly and will soon make a mistake.

Play him gently, encouraging him to make more and more wilder claims and then call his bluff.

Await your moment, it is bound to come. It could be, for example, in a meeting when a particularly risky initiative is being proposed. A quiet 'that sounds just the sort of job for Mister AYM, I'm sure he could do it' will do the trick. He won't be able to back down without losing face and, when he screws up, you can be sympathetic and understanding.

Mister Over-Promoted

This standard personality will already be over-stressed in his work. Make sure that you give him plenty of work to keep him busy. Go to him with new schemes and ideas and follow them up with frequent emails and reports.

He will probably not even realize that he's out of his depth and he will take on anything which looks as if it might advance his career. Make sure he has enough work to keep his nose to the grindstone around the clock, every minute of the day. Visit him in hospital after his nervous breakdown when you have been promoted into his job.

Mister Run-About.

This is a type found in every office. His jacket will be permanently on the back of his chair because he is always going somewhere. Full of energy, he is seen at periodic intervals running along corridors, always carrying a piece of paper in his hand. If you can stop him long enough to say a word, he will claim to be extremely busy.

He will certainly get promoted because senior management will admire his energy even though he is never trusted with any job which requires thought and planning.

He is unlikely to get further than middle management. Mister Run-About may actually be seriously deficient in real commonsense or even basic intelligence, since his work amounts to little more than that of a messenger boy.

Mister Semi-Detached

Mister SD does not appear to involve himself in office politics because he is a well-qualified mercenary who will readily move to another job if the offer is attractive enough. He is another type you should take care to befriend – he is a very good contact indeed.

You can spot him because he spends a lot of time at his desk, does not socialize and knows all the directors and top managers by their first names.

In meetings he says little or nothing, while being attentive. At some point he will move to a job where he needs a number two at a bigger salary than you are getting now. He will need someone from outside his new organization whom he can rely on. It could be you.

Mister Manic-Depressive

The Manic Depressive organization man will often have a high energy level, which has carried him so far. He will be the generator of copious new ideas and schemes. Most of his ideas are shallow, ill-thought out and are soon dropped because they have been created while his brain was in its febrile, over-active state.

He tends to be loud and forceful and to display negative emotion too easily. You are not his psychiatrist so you are under no obligation to cure him.

If he causes you problems, the direct approach is usually the best. He will already have a lot of enemies who are afraid of him, so you will get a lot of support if you out-shout him in public. Wait your moment and prepare your case well. Then don't hold back.

Mister Late Revolutionary

Beware an old man in a hurry, goes the famous saying. Energetic old men can be quite confident, even reckless in their plans. With a brilliant future behind them, they have little left to lose,

Do not cross them because they have seen more of the game than you have and they know all the tricks. Instead, become their friend and confidante because you and he will certainly have enemies in common.

Some of the other players will resent his energy and experience but he is more likely to prevail if they are stupid enough to try to join battle with him. So stay on his good side but don't make it too obvious. He will not be sticking around for long.

Mister Quiet Life.

Mister Quiet Life is serving out his time looking for as few surprises as possible. He spends his days dreaming of post-retirement fishing and gardening.

He is constantly on the lookout for ideas to crush so he will respond to any initiative you take to him with something like 'not possible, no can do' or 'I don't think that is going to work'. A good strategy for handling Mister QL is to go on to him about the benefits of retirement, meanwhile taking over his real job.

When he gets a new problem, tell him to leave it with you and wait for him to forget about it. Do this often enough and gradually you will be doing everything he should have been doing and, in time, his bosses will wonder what they are paying him for. Then he can be retired, which is what he wanted all along anyway. You are doing him a favour.

Mister Always Senior

It used to be said that every private soldier carries a marshal's baton in his kitbag. One could be promoted from the very bottom to the very top.

However, most of us do not attain the heights. The vast majority of people in white collar jobs climb the steep ladder slowly until they reach a level where further ascent is impossible or just not worth the effort. But there is a small class of people in organizations who seem never to have served in the ranks at all. Sometimes, but not always, there are plausible reasons for this, such as their having good connections like being married to the owner's daughter. But often they are people who get promoted invisibly quickly and live out their whole careers at the top table.

Often they will move from one job to a seemingly unrelated job but only at the senior level. This type never gets fired because nobody knows exactly what they do. Apart, that is, from being senior and important.

Mister No False Modesty

The most likely promotion candidate is the guy who does a good job and makes sure everyone knows about it. He is not afraid to let everyone know just how well he did.

True success creates envy and resentment so the successful braggart will have many enemies just waiting to enjoy that *Schadenfreude* moment when he falls flat on his face in public.

Mister Fixit

Mister Fixit is the person you go to privately when you get presented with a problem you have not come across before. He knows everything about the company and everyone who works there.

He is virtually fireproof because he was there before most of today's senior management. They will fear him because he could well know things about them which they would prefer to keep quiet.

He will therefore be a permanent fixture at a senior middle management level until his retirement and he is a very useful man to know.

I have used the masculine gender here so as to avoid the inelegancies of 'his/her' and its variants. It would be politically incorrect not to mention that all subspecies of the office politician come equally in both male and female forms.

7 Bosses

Good Bosses

It is a self-evident truth that anyone can be a good boss in the good times when the living is easy and there are no big problems - times when the business is going well and it is making money.

It is when the going gets tough that bosses earn their money and the good boss stands out from the bad.

If you want to get the true measure of your boss, watch him when there's a crisis in the office.

Does he rant and shout? Does he panic? Does he blame people randomly? Is his door always closed? Does he go into private meetings with a few favourite underlings?

Or does he calmly come up with a sensible plan to solve the problem? Does he involve all the staff in the solution? Does the crisis pass without a break-down of productivity and morale?

It is a sad fact that such a paragon is not a common type but, if you should meet one, you could try grabbing his coat tails by becoming his *protégé* as he ascends the corporate tree to top management.

The Peter Principle*

That universal law of corporate promotion, the Peter Principle*, declares that everyone is promoted to one

---

* See e.g. http://www.investopedia.com/terms/p/peter-principle.asp

level above their natural competence. It ensures that there are always openings for ambitious upstarts who profit from screw-ups by over-promoted managers when they get fired for incompetence.

Who can doubt its truth as a measure of human frailty when, as happens frequently, some highly placed leader figure - a top politician, maybe, or a general, a banker or even an archbishop is found to have succumbed to hubris and done something so brazenly stupid, so damagingly silly – and it usually involves some mixture of sex, politics or money - that we ordinary folk can only throw up our hands in disbelief - 'you'd have thought that someone in his position would have had more sense !'

Bad bosses

It is a sad fact that the Peter Principle means that very many bosses are over-promoted well beyond their competence level. You may have met, or you may get to meet, some of them during a career. Before you join a department you should never underestimate the importance of your new boss according to Richard Moran*

Bully Boss

> The boss's nature will have a big impact on your working life so it is important that you can work with

---

* What you Learn by Working for a Bully by Richard A. Moran, Menlo College Published on LinkedIn April 10th 2015 him/her. If your boss is a bully, then he can cause great misery to individual staff members at the same time creating a toxic atmosphere in the work environment. Employee morale will drop off with a negative effect on the efficiency and productivity of the whole operation. Once the poison is released it will spread throughout the department like an infection.

This is especially important for the inexperienced and impressionable new graduate. They may be taken advantage of because they will be intimidated by the boss's manner. They may even find themselves browbeaten into doing things they find disagreeable.

The boss's bullying nature may not be visible to senior management, says Richard Moran. To his bosses he may well come across as a very nice fellow indeed. Bullies only bully people lower down the hierarchy, although the Bully Boss will have his special favourites who will be shielded from his tirades. Moran makes four points to be borne in mind if you are thinking of joining a department where the boss is a tyrant :

1 Never underestimate how much power he is going to have over your life;

2 Bullies don't win and usually come to an unhappy end;

3 You don't need to tolerate his behaviour. You

can talk to those who can change the game plan, such as senior management.

4 Don't be a bully yourself when you become the boss. It is quite possible to be an effective boss without causing distress along the way.

Indolent Boss

Indolent Boss is an incompetent by default. He is a type of boss I have met a few times in the course of my career. This boss instinctively understands the Peter Principle and knows that he is just a little out of his depth at his rank.

His response is to do very little because he is afraid he will make a revealing mistake. To himself, he defines his role as presiding over a calm kingdom with no unpleasant surprises. He never takes the initiative or instigates any new ideas because he wants as little change as possible. New ideas may be brought to him by his underlings but he will discard or ignore most of them.

Oddly, he will sometimes excuse his lack of action by referring to himself as an 'ideas man' – a sagacious leader who provides stimulating visions for others to follow. Of course, he has never had any idea, original or unoriginal, in his life. If he tells you he is an ideas man, ask him to give you an example.

He prefers his staff to be what he may call 'low maintenance' – people who will not cause him any trouble while he sits out his tenure.

The problem with this type of boss is that his inaction leaves a power vacuum which will be filled by one of his subordinates. Sometimes this subordinate may show the management competence which the boss lacks and becomes the *de facto* leader of the pack.

Too often though, the pretender may well be the departmental troublemaker who will have free rein to get up to all sorts of mischief. It is likely that the boss will approve of the pretender and even make the troublemaker his favourite.

The boss himself will be grateful to be relieved of the responsibilities of real management. The important thing is that the pretender is keeping the boss's desk tidy regardless of the effect the arrangement is having on the rest of the workforce.

Workaholic Boss

There is a class of working human who prefers the company of his workmates to his family and the office to his home. In some cases the office may be his real home, since he spends most of his time there.

There may be good reasons for this, such as an unhappy personal life, but many workaholics are just addicted to work. It is as ingrained as a cocaine addiction.

People are not born workaholics, they grow that way, probably as a result of having to put more effort into work than the average because of limited natural ability. Workaholic Boss is not particularly more talented than his fellows. It is just that he does more and therefore he sometimes seems to achieve more, even though much of his work is 'by the book' – he is not an original thinker.

The problem with this type of individual, if you should find yourself reporting to him is that he believes that if he can work fifteen hours a day for seven days a week, then so can everyone else. In no time at all Workaholic Boss will have you getting into work at 5 am, taking work home at 10 pm and going into the office all day every Sunday.

Semi-Detached Boss

The Semi-Detached Boss is never available for decision making because he is always out of the office. He will be at meetings or on out-of-office visits.

Because he is never there to make them, important internal day-to-day decisions will get put off. Employees will become frustrated because they will not see any chance of personal self-development. His office more or less runs itself at a low level of efficiency because it is directionless.

It is a feature of the human character that we work better and happier in a disciplined regime. The discipline must not be harsh or arbitrary, of course.
But, when the functions of management – control, co-ordination, communication, planning etc – are absent, our capacity for useful work falls off quickly.

Jolly Boss

Jolly Boss may seem, on the surface to be a good person to work for. He goes to coffee and lunch with his staff, he puts on a paper hat at the Christmas party, he refers to his staff as his 'family' and he frequently proclaims that 'my door is always open'. This guy wants, too much, to be liked and he forgets the basic rule of work – that work is not part of your social life and you should never see your colleagues as friends.

At some point, Jolly Boss will need to administer discipline - a reprimand maybe, or even a dismissal. Better than looking like a Judas to the guy being fired - 'How could you? I thought you were my friend !' – it would be better if Jolly Boss had kept a proper professional distance and had not given out the wrong signals.

Managing the boss

One thing a good office politician must learn is how to manage their boss. Bosses are human beings just like you are and you need to stay on their right side. Become his/her favourite, especially if they are a high-flyer. Many great careers have been built on becoming the protégé of a successful patron.

Always remember that anyone can be flattered. Not too heavy with the flattery though! You must use subtle flattery so you don't get a reputation as a suck-up. So, it's not so much the *'...that's absolutely brilliant, sir !'*. Much better is a thoughtful *'...that's a good idea'*. Here are some basic rules for handling the boss.:

1 Always make sure your boss looks good to other people. Speak well of him when you are with people from other departments.

In meetings it is a good idea to ask his advice when one of his favourite subjects is being discussed, so that he will have an opportunity to show off his knowledge.

2 Don't take your boss problems, take him/her solutions. If you have a problem which needs his attention, don't just leave the problem with him, suggest optional solutions. If he doesn't like your ideas, then he will have a chance to correct you. For which you are grateful. (*Subtly*.)

3 Any great idea of yours which works out well was thought of first by your boss. Any idea (either his or yours) which turns out to be a flop was down to your own inexperience.

4 Your boss is always much cleverer than you are - that's why he/she is your boss and why he is paid more than you are. He may really be a muppet on the lower half of the IQ bell curve but that doesn't stop him wondering why the Nobel Prize Committee should ignore him time after time.

5 Always work late if your boss asks you to unless he is the sort of workaholic boss who expects you to put in a 150 hour week for a 40 hour salary. As a general rule, his time is infinitely precious whereas yours has absolutely no value at all.

6 Meetings need preparation so be sure you are prepared for any meeting and make sure your boss is prepared also. Prepare bullet-point executive summaries for him to take into the meeting.

7 If you can, help your boss to get promoted. Obvious really, if you want his job.

8 The boss always has the last word. Always.

How to be a boss

Bosses have their quirks and weaknesses and understanding what those are can be very useful. One of the commonest is a personality conflict i.e. whether to be popular with the workforce and liked by them or whether to be a stern taskmaster. You can't be both.

Nothing is new under the sun, as they say. The classic book on *realpolitik* dates from 1513 when Niccolo Machiavelli wrote *The Prince** at a time of political upheaval in renaissance Florence. The book is essential reading for all political animals at any level.

Among Machiavelli's pieces of advice was that a

---

* The Prince by Niccolo Machiavelli (1469-1527)

in e.g. Penguin Classics Published 1999 ISBN 0-14-044752-0

prince would be safer being feared than being loved.

Any manager needs to make the same choice, to choose carefully which of these two he wants to be. Would he prefer to be a fearsome autocrat who keeps a distance between himself and those who report to him? Or whether he wants his team to like him as a friend or a father figure?

Many bosses make the mistake of thinking that they can be both types at different times. It doesn't work that way. One just cannot be a ruthless taskmaster for most of the year and then expect to be invited to play Santa Claus at the office Christmas party.

Another piece of Machiavellian advice was that a new prince should kill off the supporters of the old regime and replace them with his own people We no longer rub out unwanted people like they did back in the sixteenth century. Instead we fire them, or move them somewhere where they are not likely to be so much of a threat.

Watch what happens in your own organization the next time a new boss is brought in. The new man needs supporters who will be grateful to him for giving them an opportunity, people whose obedience can be relied on. He may even bring his own assistants and deputies with him. He particularly does not want anyone near to him who will give him any problems such as someone who has been passed over for the very job the new man now has.

After a little time, once the incomer has his feet firmly under the table, you can expect a round of terminations or redeployments as the losers are disposed of.

8 Meetings

The people who go to meetings

One thing which every business has in common is meetings. For many in the corporate game, meetings are a source of great pleasure. They are an opportunity not to do some useful work but to spend a little time relaxing, or preening and posing. To them, meetings are a form of artistic expression, a sort of indoor street theatre.

For those characters, meetings can even become a way of life. There is a recognizable type in most organizations – he is the manager who has built his entire career around meetings.

For others, the more productive employees, meetings are distractions from whatever else they do. They would much rather be doing their regular work - they will sometimes bring it with them to the meeting.

Extrovert, confident people tend to see meetings as a chance to show off. Their introverted brothers and sisters are more likely to see meetings as ordeals to be got through as quickly as possible. But whichever personality type you are, like them or loathe them, you will not be able to avoid meetings.

At all of them a standard cast of characters can be relied on to make an appearance. They are as predictable as the characters in a pantomime.

At your next meeting, you can expect see

performances from some or all of the following *dramatis personae*:

The Professional Meeting Goer

This standard type exists in every organization. When asked how they fill their week, they will point to all the important - they are always 'important' - meetings he has been to.

The Professional Meeting Goer can be relied upon to stay silent during most meetings or make only the odd gnomic utterance – '*A good point there*' or '*I'd like to see that*'.

The Prima Donna

The Prima Donna is a self-proclaimed genius. Why, after all, would anyone not want to listen to them intone interminably as they lay down the law according to themselves?

This type needs vigorous slapping down by a strong chairman or they will get their own way by default. The rest of the meeting will often agree with them just to shut them up.

The Waffler

The Waffler is the ugly sister of The Prima Donna. What the two have in common are their attention seeking. The difference is that, instead of sticking to the point, The Waffler will waffle on about anything which slithers into their mind. If the meeting doesn't shut them up as soon as they wander off the point, because the chairman is too polite, then the whole meeting is doomed, especially if there are other Wafflers and Prima Donnas at the table waiting to add their own dribble to the proceedings.

The Abominable No-Man

There is a type of human being who likes to say 'No' to anything which might be proposed. He(or, of course, she) is a Mr Micawber in reverse, always waiting for something to turn down. Their favourite phrases are 'not possible', 'we tried that and it didn't work', 'they'll never buy it'.

They are primarily at the meeting to make sure nothing is resolved which will involve any change in their comfortable working routine. Their main aim in life is to make sure that any new idea is firmly killed off at birth.

The Opposer

This man is very similar to The Abominable No-Man except that he will always take the opposite point of view on whatever argument is being put forward.

If you put forward an argument for buying more X, then he will have an argument for buying less. If you have a well thought-out case for opening up a new market in the east, he will instantly develop an off-the-cuff argument for a new market in the west.

The difference between The Opposer and The Abominable No-Man is that The Abominable No-Man relies upon their seniority to get new ideas squashed. The Opposer, being, in their own mind, brilliantly clever, will find arguments, however thin, to try to make sure that whatever is proposed is doomed to failure.

Both types will project the public *personae* of eminent and sagacious parent figures who are carefully restraining the reckless excesses of the less experienced. This is a false front – in reality they are quiet reactionaries opposed to progress of any form.

If they are resisted, they will dig their heels in and become even more obdurate. They have spoken, so the matter is now closed. Next item Mister Chairman?

The On-The-Other-Hand

'*Seeing the bigger picture*' is the *forte* of a person who believes there are two sides to every argument and both deserve to be heard.

Essentially The On-The-Other-Hand doesn't like decision-making which explains why committees are full of his type.

A stupid group decision made by a committee of N people will have the blame shared N different ways if the decision is, in any way, risky, The On-The-Other-Hand will have abstained after arguing for both sides of the argument.

If some committee decision does actually go

belly-up, the On-The-Other-Hand character can always point out that they did, - 'look, it's in the minutes' - put the counter-argument but was out-voted.

The Last-Worder

The Last-Worder will stick, terrier-like, with a discussion to the very last word, which they are determined to have. If more than one Last-Worder is present, then discussions which start with multiple participants will gradually peter out until there are only two speakers left to fight it out for the final word. These people need cutting off before the other people at the meeting vote to kill them.

The Brown-Noser

Brown-Noser is at the meeting for a chance to brown-nose, or suck up to, the boss. If the boss is not present then Brown-Noser will probably not be there either.

Shameless, heavy brown-nosing is a terrible, distressing thing to have to watch. One wonders whether the boss himself notices it and whether he is actually taken in. With any luck the boss will despise The Brown-Noser as much as everyone else does.

Naturally, bosses need regular flattery (See Chapter 7). Being fawned upon is one of the perks of their job. The Brown-Noser simply doe not understand how to do it subtly.

The Bully-Boy

Schoolyard bullies grow up and go to work in organizations. But leopards do not change their spots. The Bully-Boy will be negative and offensive by turns, responding to any idea they dislike with a personal attack on the person speaking without sany regard for the feelings of their chosen victim.

In time, Bully-Boy's will find themselves isolated by their colleagues. But, until that happens, they use meetings to let rip with the vindictive aggression they are not allowed to exhibit in their regular office environment. If you are confronted by one of these bullies, and they are commoner than you might think, pay them back in their own coin, with raised voice, sharp tongue, personal insults and contempt. If you do, you will probably make an enemy of them but do you care? You certainly don't want to be their friend.

The Funnyman

Most organizations have at least one failed comedian who just keeps the jokes coming. These people are dangerous because they prevent serious discussion of important issues by a stream of trivial fatuous remarks. Often, since they get through so much comic material, the jokes will be sub-standard or off-color. A good way to put them down is to take exaggerated indignant personal offence at one of their remarks and then threaten to make it the basis of a formal complaint.

Useless meetings

You will not be able to avoid meetings, even if you want to. You should not want to because if you are not there, you can be certain they will agree on something to your disadvantage. After carefully dissecting your personal character flaws, of course.

Many, possibly most, meetings are simply a waste of time. Academia is famous for its pointless meetings. In my long career as an academic, I can't recall a single meeting where anything really useful was ever decided.

Decisions in universities, and, I guess, many other places, are made in advance by top management. The meeting merely rubber-stamps the boss's decision and adds a little gloss of pseudo-democracy to the decision-making process. And, of course, meetings are useful for blame-sharing, if the boss who made the decision turns out not to have been quite so infallible after all.

Why meetings fail

There are many reasons why meetings fail. The following list is not comprehensive – every organization has a different assortment of flawed individuals.

1 The people at the meeting are not taking it seriously. They arrive late, leave early, and spend most of their time doodling or playing with their *SmartPhone*'s or *iPad*'s.

2 The meeting is going on too long. Anyone's attention span is no longer than 45-50 minutes. That should be the length of a business meeting. Anything more than that and people start to lose interest in what is being said.

3 The meeting has more than its fair share of those characters listed above.

4 The meeting does not end with an action plan for every attendee. If there is no follow-up action, no one will take the meeting seriously.

Meetings should always be about doing something, not just 'talking it out'. Any meeting which does not lead to action is mere time-wasting.

Bad manners in the meeting

There is an etiquette for attending and running meetings. Make sure you are never guilty of any of the following.

1 Working during the meeting – a real no-no. It sets an example that the meeting is not important and certainly not as important as whatever else you might be doing.

2 Eating in the meeting. It used to be a fashion to have meetings over breakfast or a 'working' lunch. Eating and trying to concentrate on working is bad both for the digestion and for clear decision making.

3 Using electronic devices, texting or taking phone calls in a meeting, is just plain rude.

4 Not contributing in a meeting is also bad manners. It smacks of 'I can't be bothered with you guys'.

5 Unpunctuality is always bad form, whatever the situation. There is only ever one occasion when turning up late is acceptable and that is when a bride turns up late for her wedding.

6 Not showing up and having no excuse shows contempt for the meeting organizer.

Rules for organizing a meeting

1 Prepare well. If you are using statistics, reports or any other printed information, copies should be circulated at least three days in advance, as should the list of invitees..

2 Circulate the agenda of the meeting in good time.

3 Dress formally.

4 Start on time and do not go on too long.

5 Make sure your visual aids are set up and working. Nothing looks worse for you than amateurish presentation. Check props such as slide projectors.

6 Make sure you have someone reliable to take the minutes of the meeting so that there is an accurate written record of what was said and agreed.

7 Switch off your mobile phone and your other electronic toys. Ask all participants to do the same.

8 Participants need to have their customary seating places. If you don't know what it is then ask. The secretary of the department will know.

9 It is usual for the boss to sit at the head of the table. The more senior the employee, the nearer they will be to the boss.

10 The chair will open with a brief introduction – name and job title – of the participants.

11 Only speak when invited to by the chair.

12 Never interrupt anyone - even if you disagree strongly. Note what has been said and return to it later with the chair's permission.

13 When speaking, be brief and ensure that what you say is relevant.

14 Never discuss what was said in the meeting with anyone who was not there.

9 Negotiating

Eight rules for successful negotiation

No one ever tells you how to negotiate successfully and how to win arguments but both these two important skills can easily be learned. They are more important in the long run, than being, say, a great computer programmer or being the best in your college year at basketball.

We all want to make a success of our lives but often we see our own way forward as somehow being blocked by other people who represent a barrier, a problem.

Well, that is exactly how other people see you. You are their barrier, their problem, just as they are yours. So how do we resolve this dilemma so that both of us can move forward together?

We can negotiate with them. We can cut a deal which benefits us both. Any sale, any interview, any meeting, is a negotiation. Remember that the other guy would not be talking to you unless he wanted something.

In this kind of negotiation, do not be afraid of treating the other party as an equal. Even if the deal situation is an interview and the other guy is going to be your boss, he is not your boss yet. He is still an equal who is negotiating with you.

If you have already thought yourself into the position of subordinate, you will be giving off unconscious signals that you will be expecting to have to concede more than he will before you can close the deal. These are the eight rules.

1 Do not be afraid of your opponent. Think of the negotiation as something like judo or a game of chess. Your opponent may be a black belt or a grandmaster but the ground rules are exactly the same for both players – the so-called 'level playing field'. Do not be afraid to give it your best shot.

2 Clearly define to yourself what it is you want to get out of the deal and exactly how much you are prepared to give up to get it. Put limits on how much flexibility you can allow in your own negotiating position. Know your top line and your bottom line and stick with them

3 Concede slowly, but only in response to some concessions, maybe tentative, from the other side.

Take your time. Do not offer your own concessions too quickly. Feel your way and try to get some sense of how desperate the other side is to make a deal.

Their initial position is the top line of their wish list. For example, suppose you are negotiating your salary at a job interview. He offers his top line, twenty five thousand and you ask for seventy. He has set a bottom line, an upper limit, of forty five on what he will offer and you don't want to go below fifty five. Obviously both of you can move a little and you will eventually settle somewhere around fifty.

On the other hand, if he offers his twenty five and you ask only for fifty, then you will start working for him at thirty five.

Don't undervalue yourself !

4 When negotiating, sell your position by what they call 'blue skies' selling. Never tell your opponent how good the deal will be for you. Always tell him how good the deal will be for him.

Let me give you another example. You are buying a car. Now, the salesman thinks, if I sell this car for ten thousand dollars, I will make four thousand dollars profit.

If he were dumb enough to tell you that, then you will offer to buy it for, well, as little over six thousand as the salesman needs to feed his kids that day.

No, the salesman will stay silent on how much he hopes to make but work instead at breaking down your reluctance to buy by telling you just how much your life will be improved when actually you own this particular vehicle.

5 Remember that in a negotiation, both sides are investigating the personality of the other. Car salesmen are natural psychologists. If they can sum up a customer's personality and desires quickly then they will make their sales pitch accordingly.

The young man wants a 'babe magnet', the family man needs something safe and reliable, the retired guy is looking for economy and so on. These classifications may be rough and ready but they work for a lot of the time.

Try to see inside your opponent's head to find out what sort of person he sees you as. Then you can adjust the impression you are putting out so as to fit his opinion of what sort of stereotype he has pigeon-holed you as. This means that he will be more confident of closing the deal and he will make his concessions and get to his final offer more quickly.

6   Try to judge from verbal clues or hints, just how keen the other person is to do a deal with you. Job interview timing is a good indicator. If you are called for interview the next day, then you can be sure they are desperate to fill the job quickly.

The same applies, paradoxically, if you are not called for several weeks. This means that they have had the first round of candidates and rejected them all. Your name came up when they went through the applications a second time.

If this happens to you, you can safely assume that, if you don't screw up the interview, then the job is yours. What is more, you now have some useful information about your value in the market place.

7   What if the deal maker will not budge from their initial position? Suppose they say 'take it or leave it'. In that case, you may have to decide if their offer is worse for you than your own bottom line. If you can't do it, then simply walk away. There is always tomorrow. Make sure they know what it is you are looking for, then get up, shake hands and leave.

They will not call you back right there and then because that only happens in the movies. If they have a prepared position they will not move from, then it is likely that they are on orders from their bosses not to go any further.

So they will need time to go back to their masters to get fresh instructions. Then they could very well phone you with an invitation to meet and make a better offer. A good negotiator will recognize a call back as an opportunity to get a better deal for himself.

8 Always be ready to walk away if you think the deal will not work for you. Actually, inflexibility by your opponent is a weakness. They may be used to dealing with unskilled negotiators and therefore be used to making easy deals. If you are flexible but confident of your position, then they may re-evaluate their own negotiation starting point.

A successful negotiation will leave both parties with the feeling that they have achieved something. It is what we call a 'win-win' solution. In the car example above, the salesman might have had a bottom line of seven thousand dollars which would give him a quick thousand dollars profit. The customer might have had a top line of nine thousand – that would give him a thousand dollars off the sticker price. But if they finally agree on eight thousand, each will have done better than they were prepared to settle for and each will come out of the deal believing that they have won the contest.

How to win arguments

Sometimes, though, negotiation can spill over into argument. The basic rule is do all you can not to get into an argument in the first place. If you follow the rules about office politics, then you should be able to avoid arguments at work.

First, and most important, choose who you argue with. Don't waste your breath arguing with jerks. If someone picks a fight with you for no seeming reason, then they are a jerk. And if they are a jerk, simple insults and contempt is all the exchange requires.

If you are quick at thinking on your feet, then a sharp put-down is good. Ridicule them if you can but if you can't think of anything on the spot, an insult and a turning of your back on them will often work. They will certainly lose face if they make themselves look ridiculous by starting an argument they can't finish.

You may think of the perfect put-down too late. This is called, in French, *l'esprit d'escalier* – the wit of the staircase – what you think of after you have left the room.

Remember that cruel *riposte*. You will be able to use it again to devastating effect the next time you get into the same, or a similar, argument.

But, if you are having a serious difference of opinion with an adversary you can respect, you must apply other rules.

1 Most importantly, stay calm and do not get

emotional. Getting worked up will stop you thinking straight and will hand the advantage to your adversary. Hopefully, he will be the one who loses his cool, so do all you can to upset him.

2 Marshal your facts. What are the important bullet points about this particular subject? Most arguments come down to one or two simple facts and the different interpretations the two opponents put on them.

3 Keep your arguments simple. Do not over-elaborate your case. Stick to those one or two simple points only. For each of these points have two or three indisputable facts to back them up.

4 Avoid phrases which weaken your argument. These include *'in my opinion..', 'I submit..', 'maybe you're right but..' , 'in my view..', 'probably..', 'I'm sorry, but..' or 'this might seem a bad idea but...'* or *'I'm not an expert but...'*

All these phrases imply doubt on your part. You are defending a simple position therefore you must believe that what you are saying is absolutely correct with no room for error or disagreement.

5 Don't quote experts unless you are absolutely certain of the text and its interpretation. Your opponent may know the reference better than you do.

6 If your opponent throws some statistic at you, you can be quite certain that he is on shaky ground. Quoting statistics will weaken an argument. It is a well-known fact that 96% of people know that 83% of all statistics are made up on the spot.

7   Keep your argument free of everyday phrases which often mean the exact opposite. These include *'honest..', 'trust me..', 'you can't miss it...', 'we have plenty of time...', 'no problem...'.*

Listen out for your opponent's using them. Contradict him if he appeals to what he thinks is obvious to everyone.

8   Never argue from the particular to the general -

'You get promoted very quickly here. Look at old Smith. He went from Grade 4 to Grade 9 in just six years.'

A single example never proves a general point.

9 Don't complicate your argument with too many possibilities. 'If we had ten dollars we could go to the ball game or we could go to the movies'. If you don't have ten dollars, it doesn't matter what you would have done with it. Keep the argument simple. Listen out for phrases like 'if so-and-so then X would happen and if X happens, then Y will result.' Stick to facts, not conjectures.

10 Avoid using common words and statements which are usually used wrongly - words like 'devastated'. or 'amazing'. They are intended to intensify the strength of the message whereas, in reality, they weaken it.

Never use 'literally' emphasize a point as in *'I literally died when Smith was promoted over Jones'.*

If you win arguments it will be because you use your words in their precise sense, you avoid cliché's, you keep it simple, and you follow the basic laws of logic.

11 At the right point, let your adversary have the last word. What, I hear you say, let them win? No, if they have allowed themselves to be carried away by emotion and you have stayed calm, then letting them have the last word will make them feel guilty and remorseful once the adrenalin wears off.

They will wonder whether they have gone too far and they will not know whether they have convinced you or not. They may even think that they might have made an enemy for life, requiring an apology.

When arguments get heated

If the argument gets heated, then disappointment can be more crushing than anger. But use it very sparingly.

Always stay out of quarrels if you can but if you should find yourself drawn into one because someone has picked a fight with you, you might as well win it.

Always remember, that however much you might despise a colleague's opinions and the way he/she expresses them - you may even detest the very ground they walk on - but, and it's a very big but, you still have to work with them afterwards. Always be respectful and never force a person into a position where they have to choose between their friends and their integrity.

Let them appear to win, if that's what it takes to unruffle their feathers. You can always assume the moral high ground by being magnanimous in defeat.

It depends how important it is to you to win the argument or whether you would prefer to wait for an opportunity when you will stand a better chance of inflicting a decisive crushing defeat.

Let the other guy lose his cool !

10 Changing your job

The standard career path

A sensible boss will need to make sure that success is rewarded. He will promote successful employees regularly or his best staff will leave. If promotion is too long in coming, the first ones to go will be the most valuable employees, those who possess the most marketable and useful skills.

If you are competent, you should be able to look forward to a reasonable career path in an organization with regular promotions as you gain more experience and add more value to the company.

If you stay with the same company for your whole career from graduation at, say, age twenty two, then you will be a trainee or apprentice for the first year followed by a junior management position with regular steps up the ladder until, by your early thirties, you can be expected to have joined middle management.

By middle management, you will be, maybe, a supermarket or hotel manager. If you are in the finance industry, you may be a retail bank branch manager or an investment manager with a sizeable client portfolio. You will be in charge of a small team who report to you.

Between thirty and forty is when you make the move from middle to senior management. This is when you might need to extend your educational background with an MBA.

By forty, with a clean record and no screw-ups you should be aiming for senior management if you are not there already. Once you are over that hurdle, then the sky's the limit. How far you go is just a matter of personal ability and good health.

Promotion

The organization which has been in the management hierarchy business the longest and therefore knows how to do it best is the military. Armies have had millennia to get the model right. Most well-run large organizations echo the military management structure.

Military ranks are divided into three levels – strategic, tactical and operational or, in civilian life, senior, middle and junior management.

In the army, senior management is all those ranks from full colonel to top general. In peacetime, they have a five to ten year event horizon, which is to say that their decisions will not impact on the organization for that number of years.

Middle management is all the other officers up to the rank of lieutenant-colonel. Their corresponding scope is about one year. Middle management decisions are mainly about resources or, as the military calls them, logistics.

Operational or junior management are the NCO's who handle decisions on a day-by-day basis.

So it is in big companies or the public sector. Their management structures usually closely follow the military model. Promotion to major or lieutenant-colonel is fairly automatic provided one keeps one's nose clean. The big step is going higher than that.

A company will apply many of the same rules as the military when it comes to promotion. There will be annual assessments of performance based upon the completion of assigned tasks. Promotions will be made regularly and, if an officer proves good enough then he can expect periodic advancement.

What the army also does is to promote an officer and then post him/her to a new location so that the new promotee is not compromised when it comes to exercising authority over his previous equals.

Many large multinational companies work the same sort of system – promotion and posting. Turning down a promotion because it would mean a posting to some uncongenial location is, naturally enough, a career-terminating decision.

If you are going to get near the top of say, a large oil company, then you will certainly have to serve time in some unpleasant dangerous places because those are where the oil is usually found.

You can expect to be spending periods of up to five years or more in some of them while you are being tested for further advancement.

Some organizations, for example, the US State Department, prefer their male officers to be married, and preferably to foreign wives who will go to new foreign locations more readily than American wives, who will be more likely to stand in the way of a posting to a difficult or dangerous country. .

If regular relocation is one of the rules of your chosen employer then you should know what you have taken on.

The promotion lottery

For those working in smaller concerns, promotion is often a matter of playing the office politics more adroitly than your competitors. Befriending the boss sometimes works, especially if he awards promotions like Christmas presents. (See Chapter 7)

This 'gift' approach to promotion, if that is the style, is very unfair on honest toilers who might not be aware that there is an inner clique who are going to get all the prizes every time. It is a mark of amateur management, usually management which has been self-taught on the job. But if that's the way it is done in your place of work, it is best to join the inner cabal ASAP.

If there is no sign of cronyism, then it may be because the boss is too remote from his underlings. But his promotions will still follow a pattern. You should watch carefully and try to work out what the promotion style is for future reference.

Some bosses, the ardent feminists, will only promote women on principle, since promoting an inferior woman over a superior man is striking a blow in the struggle for female equality.

Other bosses will also only promote women if they are young and pretty. If you are in a setup where promotion is dependent on sexual favours, and yes, they still do exist, then you have a choice to make. As a woman you have the choice of joining the frolics, staying unpromoted or moving on. If you are a man, you have the choice of moving on or, well, moving on.

Many bosses will not promote anyone they consider a threat. An insecure boss, possibly aware that the job is just a little beyond him, will not promote some sharp young upstart who will make him look even worse. He will go instead for the dullard or the plodder.

Far better to have a second-rate yes-man than some potential high-flyer who will highlight his own shortcomings, is how he thinks.

If that is what your boss is like and it is clear that he is only ever going to promote the mediocre, then mediocrity is a simple enough role to play if you want promotion badly enough.

Transferring to another department

Once you have worked out your departmental setup, you may decide that you are not ever going to get the boss's job. Maybe the boss has already come to the end of the career road and is only batting out a very long time to retirement.

If you are stuck with a boss who is immovable or too difficult to work with then a transfer is a possible way out. Ask around discreetly to see which other departments have a boss with a better attitude and work at getting a transfer there. Choose, if you can, a department where the head is nearing retirement.

Moving on – the gagging clause

The only other option is to get another job. Move on. By now you should have a network of useful contacts as well as a lot of inside information about your present company which will be of great value to a competitor. So you will be in a strong trading position.

Most companies will impose a 'gagging clause' on their employees, a non-disclosure agreement which prevents them passing on information to a new competitor company for a period after they resign.

You could ignore it, if breaking it will get you a better job elsewhere. One of life's most liberating phrases is 'let them sue me'. In reality, ex-employees are rarely sued for breaking employment contracts. Let me give you a couple of examples.

It is well known that some of the best paid people on the planet are in charge of bank databases. In the same way that the Sultan of Turkey's head guard was allowed a big harem himself, bank database managers are paid silly money because, well, these days, money is bits and bytes and those guys are in charge of the whole tin box, billions of the stuff.

But they are just human beings after all, and even though they are already paid more than most honest employees, they still want more. Since they have the key to the money box, then what is more natural than they should want to join the billionaire set by helping themselves to a little of what they are paid to guard? I'll bet that the Sultan's head gamekeeper felt exactly the same. That's what human beings are like.

Now suppose the bank finds out that a million or three of electronic cash has gone walkabout and the database manager is now living well above his pay grade, what should they do?

Call in the cops, have the guy arrested and put on trial so that he can tell the world that the bank has an insecure computer system? No, no, no, that would be deeply stupid.

Better, far better, would be to give him three months salary and a good reference and then escort him off the premises. With luck he should be able to get himself a database administrator's job with a competitor bank.

Another example of how 'non-disclosure agreements' are systematically ignored occurs when employees of government departments with large budgets are ready to move on.

In theory, the Departments of Health and Defense or any department with a large IT budget, are entirely independent of the large supplier companies - the pharmaceutical giants, the defense contractors and the large software houses.

In practice though, there is a close warm symbiotic relationship between the major suppliers and those in charge of government purchasing. There is what is called a 'revolving door'.

Retiring senior civil servants and politicians from the departments which make the expensive purchases are instantly snapped up by the big companies precisely for their knowledge of government procurement intentions. The retirees may actually have deliberately framed departmental policies themselves in anticipation of a lucrative second career after they have left public service.

Playing the loyalty card

There is a little drama that is always played out whenever an employee, especially a valuable employee, decides for his own good that it is time to go. Consider, for example, when a valuable software engineer, tired of working for below the market rate and passed over for promotion, decides to move on. He has used the present company to hone skills which are not easy to come by on the open market.

You cannot just put a small ad. in the local newspaper or whistle out of the window for an experienced, let us say, C++ software designer with deep experience of real-time online applications and a wide knowledge of the construction industry.

Such people are rare. The ideal replacement may not want to move from his present job and the other four people in the country who might possibly fit the bill aren't interested either.

The person on the move will work off his two/three months notice while the boss decides what to do. The advert goes out and attracts no suitable candidates – just a bunch of no-hopers. The advert is repeated again and again at great cost and potential possibles are invited for interview, also at great cost.

All this takes time until maybe, a half-way satisfactory

appointment is made. But the new guy will need a higher salary than the company has been used to paying. Moreover, he will need relocation costs and he will also need to work out his own three months notice. Once in post, the new man will not be up to full speed right away. He will need time to find his feet .

The whole process of getting the new programmer in place and fully productive will take up to a year, during most of which time the work will have been on hold, possibly to the benefit of the company's competition.

What a lot of new graduates may not appreciate is just how much each employee contributes to the profit of a successful company.

Losing a high-value employee can be very expensive even to a large and successful organization For example, in the reporting year 2014, the airline British Airways employed 20,671 employees and made an operating profit of €762million. That is an average contribution from each employee of €36,863*.

That average figure is not distributed evenly across the entire workforce. Some employees will generate very much higher revenue than others. These higher value employees are the people who will generate most of the overall profit. But they are also the people who are most likely to be poached by rival companies. It makes perfect sense to renumerate them properly.

Faced with the loss of one of these more valuable a

---

*http://www.telegraph.co.uk/finance/newsbysector/transport/1066682 2/British-Airways-owner-IAG-flies-back-into-black.html
http://www.telegraph.co.uk/finance/newsbysector/transport/8167505/ British-Airways-Iberia-merger-by-numbers.html

company may decide to play the loyalty card. They will try to appeal to the departing employee's company loyalty, ignoring the fact that, in different circumstances, they would not show any loyalty in return.

Let us suppose, for the sake of argument, that this valuable software engineer is earning $60,000 a year. So to sweeten the deal, he will be offered, if he stays, a raise to $70,000, because any new person they hire will need the industry going rate, which is now $90,000.

Yes, the departing employee should answer when they put this deal to him, if I am worth seventy now, why wasn't I paid seventy yesterday?

Employee should regularly measure their salary and benefits against the varying industry standard. One thing which happens is 'salary drift'. If you stay with one company long enough, you will find your financial rewards dropping below the industry norm for the job you are doing.

This is because annual raises and salary reviews frequently make awards below the rate of inflation. Even if they were to give you raises in line with general inflation, you should be getting salary increases above that to take account of your increased experience and value to the company, which may well be, as illustrated by the British Airways exmple, quite considerable.

Your employers may think that because you are a middle manager being paid a decent middle-class salary, then that is all it takes to satisfy you. They, the top management, who might be paid tens of times more than you are, will still think themselves as bestowers of munificent *largesse* on those employees who are earning them their fortunes.

These are simple facts of life. If you are being underpaid and you can't negotiate a higher salary then move somewhere where you will be appreciated. If you are offered more to stay then you might consider rejecting the offer because they have been underpaying you and they hoped you wouldn't notice. Loyalty is an emotion and this is emotionless business where you trade your skills and labour in the market place in return for the very best price for yourself.

Remember, if your organization wanted to fire you on the spot at five minutes' notice they would do so whatever it says in your contract. Who can afford to file a wrongful dismissal case against a big company?

Walking out

If you really hate the place where you work and you see no future there, do not just walk out, however tempting that may be. Instead, start calling in your favours from your network to get another job. It is always much easier to get another job if you are employed already. Only after your new employment contract is signe will you be in a position to let your present boss know exactly where he can insert his job.

If you do leave, remember that you may be surrendering useful paid notice or even benefits. As you get health scheme payments and pension benefits become more important than salary.

Companies usually prefer their employees to be

married which means that they will be in debt with mortgages and school fees, all of which make moving so much harder. From a company's point of view, the ideal employee is a workaholic 40 year-old with house payments, children and a career spouse.

Often companies will offer cheap loans to important staff members to keep them indebted. Not only is their money safe but the wage-slave is now even more unlikely to move. It is the twenty first century equivalent of the tied cottage.

A popular way to reward employees and to ensure loyalty is to give them shares in the company as an annual bonus. The employee then feels that he actually has a stake in the fortunes of his employers and will be more motivated to work even harder. The issuing of small numbers of shares in place of cash is virtually cost-free for the company which gains considerable employee loyalty in return for virtually zero outlay.

Many companies, especially in high-tech industries like information technology, will employ qualified people so that the competition can't have them. Some large successful companies scour the American universities for the very best talent and then employ it at generous wage rates.

By all means change jobs for promotion or better pay but be careful not too move too often. Ideally, a move every 3-5 years is about right. Changing jobs every couple of years looks unreliable, that you are someone who is afraid to commit to the work. Staying too long in one job gives the opposite impression of someone who is too over-cautious and conservative.

11 Dressing for Success

How you look matters

Your personal presentation is critically important for success in life because it is the outward statement you make about yourself on a continuous basis.

It is amazing how many people do not understand this basic fact. Good grooming, being well-dressed and good personal hygiene are essentials if you are intending to make it in your career. This is equally true for men and women.

Hair must be well cut, shoes must be polished, clothes must be pressed and fresh. You must always present yourself to the very highest standard you can attain.

Buy the best you can afford

Your clothes should be the best that you can afford. You should be investing at least 5%, better 10%, of your disposable income in them on a continuous basis if you are to build up a decent wardrobe. For both men and women, a dozen suits of good cut is the eventual target to be aimed at.

This is expensive so you must acquire them slowly. It takes time. But they are a good investment, one of the best you will ever make, so buy carefully and slowly and only buy the best you can afford. You should start with what you can afford and add to it bit by bit as you go along. It may take a few years but you should always think about trading up and replacing the cheaper stuff with something better.

Money spent on clothes may seem like an extravagance but it will repay itself many times over, I promise you. Clothes are a far better investment than, for example, a car.

Why dress up at work?

There is a false belief that formal dressing for an interview or even for a normal day at work is somehow 'not being yourself'. Well, my friend, that is the whole point. You are not being 'yourself'. When you go to work, you are playing a role, you are on display.

No-one is interested in the 'yourself' inside your formal wear. They, the people who write your pay check have no interest in the 'real' you, they just want you to work profitably and efficiently for them.

And as we have said, your colleagues are your competitors - presenting yourself better than them is just part of the office contest.

But there are still people who don't get it. Like the character who dresses like a bum with a 'take me as I am, I'm not going to change' attitude. Well, buddy boy, if that's what you think, then I'll see you in the dole queue.

A lot of people, men especially, have the mistaken notion that, by dressing down, they are somehow expressing a free and independent spirit - that casual clothes are, somehow, an assertion of individuality.

That is the very opposite of the truth, even if you do have an individuality which is worth asserting. If everyone is dressing as if for a night at the pub, where's the free spirit in conforming to what everyone else is doing?

As a new graduate at work, you must not fall into the trap of thinking that you can continue to dress the same way you did at college. A formal suit is OK for the interview but don't think that once you have got the job, you can revert to the way you dressed at college. No you can't. Work is a new world, a step change from being a student. Do it right from day one.

You may feel more comfortable dressed in what was OK at college but it just will not work in the corporate world.

Business dressing for men

Suits

Some famous writers have pointed out that it is the well-dressed man, the man who stands out from the crowd because he is well-dressed, who is making the truly rebellious statement. What's more, if you look good then you'll feel good. If you feel good then you'll perform better in the work arena.

Successful men wear suits at work. Bums and losers wear what they fancy without regard for what other people think. A man should get used to used to wearing suits. He should look and feel comfortable in them. If the man is not a natural suit wearer, then, as the old saying has it, it will look as if the suit is wearing him instead of the other way around.

Suits need to be cleaned and pressed regularly. Ideally, a suit should only be worn once a week and then hung for a couple of days before it is pressed. A suit should be dry-cleaned after a dozen or so wearings. It is your office armor, so to speak, so treat it well.

Ideally your suits should be bespoke. Off-the-peg suits just do not quite ever fit properly. A suit looks good only if it has been cut to the wearer's personal shape.

If you are a new graduate, then you are not going to be able to afford made-to-measure. A couple of store-bought suits is where you start from. Two is the minimum because you should never wear the same suit two days running.

As you start to earn money, you might like to try

some of the online far-eastern tailors who will measure you up and send the measurements back to Hong Kong for making up. They will turn them around in a week or two at a tenth of the cost of Savile Row and the suits will look good because they will fit properly.

Suits for work should always be dark blue or dark grey, certainly in winter. During the summer, lighter colours are permissible. Not too light – linen summer suits are OK for holidays but wrong for a day at the office.

Anyway, linen loses its shape immediately you put it on so unless you are auditioning for a remake of 'Casablanca', leave your lightweight summer suits at home.

Shirts and neckties

Shirts should also be made-to-measure. You will need at least a dozen in a complete wardrobe. This might sound a lot, but made-to-measure monogrammed shirts from Thailand or The Philippines can be yours for less than half the cost of the store-bought ready-to-wear versions in the West.

The wearing of neckties seems to be going out of fashion. This is a strange trend. A suit without a necktie is a look now even favoured by the powerful and famous. I saw on TV the Presidents of the USA and Russia together at the G8 summit looking oh-so-casual in their expensive suits but without neckties. It was not a pretty sight.

Tie-less is a fashion I disapprove of because it looks

scruffy, especially on an old man whose wrinkled neck would be far better hidden behind a stylish necktie.

Build up a collection of good neckties, preferably silk. Immediately throw away any tie which picks up a stain.

Never, never, never wear a bowtie unless it is black and you are also wearing a tuxedo. Bowties with a business suit are for those sad characters who fancy themselves as raffish or intellectual. When you are at work you need to blend in, while simultaneously emanating a slight air of bespoke superiority.

Shoes

Shoes are very important. When a doorman at some exclusive fancy restaurant or nightclub is sizing up a man who wants to get in, he will always look at two things, the man's shoes and his watch.

Good shoes are very important as well as being more comfortable than cheapoes. They are also much better value. You can buy a cheap pair of shoes for, say $75, which will be agony to break in and which will have six months life at the most.

But if you can afford to spend $500 on a good pair from a reputable maker, they will last at least ten years and look as good, or even better, as they get older. They are also more economical since quality shoes can be repaired – the cheap ones are just thrown away.

Brown shoes look richer than black. Grey suits pair well with brown shoes but never, of course, match brown shoes with a blue or black suit.

You will need to build up to about five pairs of shoes

for a basic wardrobe. Do not wear the same pair two days running. Take them off the moment you get in at night and put shoe trees in them.

Naturally I don't have to tell you to clean them well with wax polish at least once a week. Your belt, always leather, never artificial, should approximate to the colour of the shoes.

Jewellery

Don't overdo the jewellery. For men, decent but not gaudy cufflinks – plain gold or silver if your budget runs to it - look so much better than buttoned cuffs. Save up for a good watch. Do not be ostentatious when it comes to your watch, just demonstrate your discreet good taste, but buy wisely, the best you can afford.

A cheap watch or some counterfeit copy of a designer brand will be worth precisely zero about ten minutes after you first put it on. A genuine quality timepiece will hold its value over a lifetime.

Unless you are a drug dealer or a Formula One racing driver, avoid those heavy, wrist-breaking, flashy timepieces with multiple dials.

A plain wedding ring or signet ring is OK but no more than that. Other accessories for men should include a good pen – it says so much more about you than a 10 cent disposable. Your wallet should be slim and sexy – made of fine leather but big enough to hold all you need.

If you intend to go to work wearing one of more earrings, be sure you are a woman.

Business dressing for women

If a man really wants to know how he should dress and present himself, he just has to ask any woman. Women understand the basic rules of self-presentation far better than men because they put so much more effort into it. A woman knows that work is not a chore to be got through as easily as possible without much thought or effort.

It is an opportunity for self-display, full of subtle but important games of one-upmanship which are driven by undercurrents of intense competition. In time, men learn these rules too, but, almost from birth, women understand the importance to be placed on appearance and style.

A woman will always know also the cost of another woman's wardrobe down to the last penny. Women can smell Gucci and Prada from a mile away.

Women's clothes should be well-cut in good quality fabrics. A business suit in subfusc colours always looks good. It should be tailored with a knee-length or calf-length skirt. Trouser suits look professional. Naturally, a woman, like a man, should have a selection of suits so that the suit will always look 'fresh' i.e. clean and well-pressed.

Your clothes should be made from natural materials such as cotton, wool, silk and leather - but go easy on the leather unless you are looking for an invitation to an S-M party !

Anything which reveals cleavage, midriff or thighs is definite 'no-no'.

YES   NO

At work, women should dress conservatively

Displays of skin might be seen as provocative which might offend some company clients.

Blouses should be clean and pressed without revealing necklines.

Many companies prefer women to wear tights or stockings even in warm weather.

Shoes should be low-heel without open-toes. High heels are generally a no-no in many outfits as well as being uncomfortable when they are worn continuously over a long working day. Leather shoes look better than shoes made from man-made material. They should match the rest of the outfit.

Do go easy on the scent.. Apply scents sparingly because some people have allergic reactions to them. Others associate strong perfumes with provocative women. Personally I don't hold that opinion but your co-workers may well do. they are common prejudices.

Makeup should be discreet. Your hair should be clean, cut regularly and brushed.

Women can be a little freer with the jewellery but it should be good jewellery, never flashy costume baubles. Earrings should be discreet; never those vast hoops which make a woman look like a fairground fortune teller.

For both men and women, the message is the same. At work one should dress conservatively with style. Always buy the best clothes you can afford and look after them – they are your camouflage at the workplace battleground.

12 Managing your money

Getting real about money

Personal finance and how to manage one's money - so-called 'financial literacy' – should be core subjects in school and college. In my country, the UK, financial literacy only recently became part of the high school curriculum. The classes are being delivered by local retail banks, who are not exactly disinterested.

Money management will cost the average college graduate more time and heartache than almost any other part of life apart from sex and personal relationships. And, like sex and personal relationships, the young person usually has to learn how to do it by trial and error and bitter experience. No one teaches you.

Maybe that is because, like sex, older people are embarrassed, not so much at the mechanics of money and sex, which are simple enough, but because they are, likely as not, ashamed of their own mistakes at both activities. Ignoring these two vitally important parts of everyone's life makes the job of educators that much simpler - they just don't teach sex and they just don't teach money !

It is no wonder that the newspapers are full of stories of people who manage to screw up big time in both departments, screw-ups which so many people find fascinating - 'there but for the grace of God, go I'

When it came to money, I made all the mistakes possible because no-one taught me about money, probably because my parents didn't know about money themselves and that was because they had never had any. But the cycle has to stop somewhere and for all those who can learn from my experiences, this is what I have to pass on.

Making the most of your salary

So, since we have not been born rich, nor do we have riches thrust upon us, we have to make the best of whatever money comes our way. Managing money is harder when you don't have so much of it.

Let us start with some incontrovertible facts of life.

1 *Most of us work at jobs.*
2 *Jobs provide wages or salary and benefits.*
3 *Benefits are very important. Especially as one gets older.*
4 *Money earned is what keeps us alive. Managing it is one of the most important things we have to do.*
5 *Money can slip away easily.*

We have already established that you are not going to get rich because you don't have a talent for getting rich. Nor are you going to become a famous sportsman or entertainer. It is a job which is going to provide most of us with the fundamentals of life. Benefits are nice as well, that is to say, pension, sick pay, medical cover and so on.

If you are young and strong, then do not be tempted into ignoring the benefits because you will be old very soon. It comes around distressingly quickly.

Our money is precious. What little money we have must be looked after very carefully because it can soon slip away like quicksilver.

Savings

So, practical steps, what do you need to do? If you are a wage earner then, from day one, you must start saving regularly. Save as much as you can and never less than ten percent of your net pay. Do it now ! Open a savings account, and keep those payments going in, month after month.

The trailer parks and squatters dens are full of people who once had good jobs and did not provide for their futures. Someone once said that we are never more than two pay checks away from living on the streets. That means that you need to build up a cushion of a few months salary just in case you lose your job.

But, you may think, my job is safe, I am not going to be fired or made redundant. Not so, if your company hits a rough patch they may fire you there and then without a moment's regret.

If you are a couple, you should live on the larger salary and save the smaller one because the effect of losing both jobs at the same time will be proportionately worse. And couples pretty soon become three or four or more, so no sooner are you out of college than you have new college fees to plan for.

For most people, there are regular monthly bills and living expenses and those must be paid first. If there is anything left at the end of the month then that is what is saved. This is entirely the wrong way of doing it. The savings must come first. You should regard the saving from your salary as paying yourself. What you have been doing is paying the butcher and the baker and the candlestick maker before you paid the guy who earned the money in the first place.

> Instead of :   *Savings = Income − Expenditure,*
> it should be : *Expenditure = Income − Savings.*

In other words, trim your expenditure to what is left of your income after the essential savings have been put in the bank.

The good news is that your savings will grow quickly. Let's look at the math.

Suppose you take home $30,000 a year and you save 10% of it in a bank account which pays 2% net interest every year for twenty years. Let us suppose also that you get a modest raise of 2% a year.

Then your take home pay after twenty years will be $43,700. But your savings will be $87,400, which is a cushion of two years' salary to give you time to get another job. (You will still be in your forties.).

Do you need to live poor while you are working and saving? No, of course not, but always remember, ten per cent, ten per cent !

Be sure to start saving from day one

Keeping track of your money

Another thing you should always do is to keep good accounts so that you know where your money is going. I used to be a real klutz with money until electronic spreadsheets came out in the 1980's. That is when my financial life turned around. It worked for me and it can work for you too. These days I use Microsoft Excel like half the world does.

There are some excellent ways to waste money, to see it drain away. Going on shopping sprees to buy things you don't need is one of them. The shopping malls are full of 'stuff' which you don't, I promise you, need. Well you didn't need it before you saw it, did you?

Always ask yourself, before you buy, 'do I really need this?' Nine times out of ten the answer will be no, so just forget it. The world is full of people who want to make a quick buck by inventing useless stuff for other people to buy.

If you must buy something then you should always buy the best of its quality you can afford. It will last longer than cheap stuff. Cheap jewellery, cheap clothes, cheap furniture are all false economies.

But buying trash is not the only way you can burn away your money. There are also smoking, gambling, drugs, drink and the lottery.

And what about the latest super-duper 4x4 must-have, look-at-me, fancy set of wheels which you really need, man, like really. Well, man, you don't need it, like really.

Let me tell you that big fancy cars impress no one. It used to be said that the big car was a status symbol. If they ever were status symbols, they certainly aren't now when driving on over-crowded roads is a real ordeal.

A car is just another piece of domestic hardware, carrying no more status than the model of your washing machine. That is not to say that a fancy car doesn't make a statement about its owner. It certainly does, it tells the world 'Look at me ! I'm an idiot ! I've got more money than sense !'.

If you must buy a car, buy the cheapest smallest model which will do the job of getting you from A to B. Second hand is better than new because new cars depreciate in value, literally exponentially.

Borrowing and debt

Try not to have to borrow money, and certainly never borrow money to fund day-to-day personal consumption. If you can do without a credit card then do so. They are a temptation to overspend. Of course, they are very convenient and I do have one myself. But I always make sure that I pay the balance off regularly each month so that I am not building up a debt.

Credit card interest rates at 1-2% per month may sound small but they are actually quite ruinous when averaged over a year. One must be very disciplined if one is not to get into the long-term trap of credit card debt.

Even worse are pay-day loans which are no more than legitimized criminal loan-sharking. Annual interest rates to pay-day loan companies can run into thousands of percent. They are only for the very desperate.

Good borrowing

Not all borrowing is a bad idea. It is OK to borrow when:

1 The loan is for an investment which will improve your financial position; Buying a house, for example,

is a better idea than renting because houses usually appreciate in value. Investing in a mortgage instead of paying rent, usually makes sound financial sense.

2 The interest rate is containable. This is why credit cards are a bad idea for long term borrowing – the interest rate per annum may be as high as 20-30%.

Ask yourself, if someone offered to sell you a dollar bill for one dollar twenty cents, you wouldn't take the deal now, would you? That's what borrowing on a credit card is.

3 The loan can be repaid within a reasonable time. You want to see some light at the end of the tunnel.

4 The loan can be repaid without harsh penalties. Read the small print. Many money lenders add penalty clauses of one or more repayments on top of the amount outstanding. Your circumstances may change and you may want to get the usurer off your back. Check that it would not be too expensive in terms of penalties for early repayment.

5 The repayments are within your budget surplus. Never borrow so much that the monthly repayments are crippling. As a rule of thumb regarding the two biggest monthly payments, your mortgage repayments should not be more than about 25% of your income and your car payments should be less than 10%. Both figues for your net income after you have saved the first 10%, of course.

Bad borrowing

It is stupid to borrow when:

1 The loan is for everyday consumption;

2 The interest rate is too high, like 'payday' loans;

3 The repayment period is too long;

4 There are heavy penalties for early repayment;

5 The repayments will take too much out of your monthly budget so that you will have difficulties meeting basic living costs.

Who wants to be a millionaire?

Do you want to be rich? We have all had the dream from time to time. After all, being rich requires no more effort than being poor. Being poor is a constant struggle to balance the budget and make ends meet. Poverty takes time and effort. Being rich also takes time and effort, just less time and different kinds of effort.

First of all, let's define 'rich' and 'wealth'. How much does it take before you feel 'rich'? A million dollars? Ten million?

Much less than that. Do you need a Ferrari, or a palace? Do you need champagne at $100 a bottle when you prefer beer anyway? But the dream lives on – if you are rich you will be happy because you are a success in the eyes of the world.

I am not rich, although I have known some rich people. They were, for the most part quite ordinary - dull in many cases. They had mostly come by their wealth slowly. Many were millionaires, a debased currency when the new world standard for avarice is now 'billionaire'. Soon it will be 'trillionaire' as inflation works its deadly effect.

But to be a millionaire is a good start. Well, a millionaire is not so special. Anyone with a few houses inherited from grandparents is a millionaire. Add into that a pension fund and a few investments and there you are – more money than you can spend unless you take up serious drugs or use fifty dollar bills to light your Havana cigars. So, what are the rules? They are quite simple. Here, for what it is worth, is what I have observed of the rich.*

1 You do not have to invent something original to be rich. The Internet has made a lot of people rich but not all of them had an original idea.

I am always intrigued by the well-known story about the nineteenth century California gold rush. A very few made money from panning for gold but the the guys who really struck it rich were the ordinary traders who sold the shovels and the pickaxes to the prospectors.

---

* A good book to read is 'The Rules of Wealth' by Richard Templar (Pub. Pearson Education Ltd., 2007, ISBN 978-0273-71019-2.

If you really want to make money, don't look for an elusive crock of gold. Something ordinary will do it. For example, just become the best plumber in your city.

2 Be physically near where the money is. You will make more money as a lowly wage slave on Wall Street looking for an opening than you will make as a big shot in Nowheresville.

This rule can be bent slightly these days when the Internet lets us trade profitably from anywhere in the world and the multinational companies have branches everywhere. But, on the whole, the rich tend to hang out with the rich.

3 Better to get into a business which will bring steady profits for many years than look for that one big score. If you want to make money in business, the best things to get into are what people will always want – food, energy, sex, alcohol, entertainment.

And of course land. Someone once asked Bob Hope, the great American comedian, how to get rich. He replied that it is easy. What you do, he said, was to drive to the edge of the city where suburbs stop and the desert begins. Then buy every square yard of desert you can see. Land, they've stopped making it, and people, they just keep getting more and more.

4 If you have an exceptional special talent for something, then work on that. If you are good enough at what you can do, the money will appear. It

up your own business must be the way to riches.

This is not always the case. It is true that very successful businessmen make a lot of money but then so do some very well-paid employees working in companies owned by other people. For example, the millionaire stockbrokers and hedge fund traders are employees. They do not own the firms or the banks they work for.

New businesses are difficult to get going

Many, probably most, businesses do not flourish and prosper. The attrition rate is very high - a business which can be considered viable is one which still has its head above water two years after start up.

The first year or two are crucial to the long term success. Typically, for this introductory period, money will be going out faster than it is coming in because it takes time to build up a client base.

This period is often termed 'Death Valley', the period when the profits curve stays resolutely below the axis even though the business partners still have to eat and pay their bills. It is also when major outlays need to be made - there will be capital equipment to buy and there may be set-up taxes to pay.

One of the reason for casualties in Death Valley is because many start-up businesses are under-capitalized and that is because the business plan will have been over-optimistic. It wiill have underestimated the size of the outgoings and overestimated the income the enterprise will be bringing in to pay for them. Many business plans do not allow a contingency for the unexpected expense which can devastate a tight budget. When that happens, the magic moment of breakeven will seem like a distant over-the-rainbow dream.

Plunging headlong into a new business is only for the very brave or the very foolish. If you are thinking of going it alone you will still need an income sufficient for your living expenses while you are building up your new enterprise..

If you can run your business while keeping your day job so that the new business is little more than a hobby, then you will have more chance of success, or at least a smaller chance of failure, than if you bet all your severance pay or your life savings on becoming the next Mark Zuckerberg.

Do you need an original business idea?

You do not need a novel idea to be a business success. It stands to reason that your business will have more likelihood of survival if it is in some business area where people are already making money. The trading patterns and customer base will be better understood than for some novel enterprise which no one has tried before.

People are, on the whole, conservative and new ideas need time to take hold. If there is a niche for an old-fashioned business then you might be able to fill the void. For example, if your town does not have a wine shop and people need to travel to buy their supplies, then opening a wine shop will carry some potential for success. There will be a ready-made customer base. On the other hand, novel business ideas come with a lot of hit-and-miss exploration of where the market is to be found.

To illustrate this, consider e-commerce. Even after more than twenty years, the right way to run many online businesses is still not fully understood. Many once promising Internet businesses have gone bust because the entrepreneurs did not understand where they would find their client base.

Many still don't. A good example of this is the publishing industry – newspapers and books. Some conventional publishers have still not come to terms with the digital revolution and how to adapt to it. Newspapers, for example, must produce free online versions to stay visible even when they are losing money on their hard copy sales.

Can you turn your hobby into a business?

Another mistake which would-be entrepreneurs make is to go into a business which is an extension of their hobby. A classic case is the restaurant set up by someone who likes cooking. This is definitely the wrong reason to become a catering entrepreneur.

The restaurant trade is a cut-throat business which requires large initial capital investment and high continuous overheads in return for slim margins gained against ruthless competition. It has little to do with cooking nutritious and tasty meals for your friends and family.

If you do make a go of your new business, for example, with the wine store above, you will not be able to sit back and be left alone to develop it unopposed.

Once the major wine suppliers see that you have found a gap in their network, they will immediately open a store in competition to you and do their best to drive you out of town. That's the way capitalism works.

The little guy may only be making peanuts but the big guys, with their money and their supply networks, will do whatever they need to do to take those peanuts off him.

Are you an inventor?

Suppose you really do have a great idea which, you think, will transform the world as much as Microsoft *Windows* did. Well, the first thing to note is that many other people are having exactly the same idea as you are having and they are having it right now, at this very minute.

When Orville and Wilbur Wright changed the world in 1903, they were not alone, developing a revolutionary idea which only they had ever thought of. No, many other people were also in the race to bring the first heavier-than-air machine to market.

Does anyone remember the also-rans who also invested as much time and effort and cash into the dream of flight? The Wrights got there first, that was all. They got the fame and the glory and the applause of history. Their competitors, not so far behind them, got nothing. Who knows their names now?

Original ideas are off the menu unless you have the sort of investment capital to beat off all the opposition. I know this from first-hand experience when I set up a small company to market my garden design software in the early 1990's. We were the first to market. Well, first by about fifteen minutes. Then we suddenly found that we had a dozen competitors.

This was not necessarily a bad thing. The more people there are out there advertising similar products, the more potential customers will be made aware of a novel type of product.

Unfortunately, among the competitors were several big companies with big money who could simply steal our idea and our tiny profits.

It was a sorry lesson. I have had a couple of businesses since then, but I was always careful to make sure that I had a real income to fall back on. By all means set up your own business if that is what appeals to you. But in my experience, the rewards will only come slowly, if at all. Don't give up the day job.

What does it takes to run a business?

Alison Green is a well-known management consultant who writes a famous blog*. According to her, successful entrepreneurs need five basic personal abilities. They need, she says :

1 The ability to manage their time. Starting a new business is 24/7 at least eight days a week. If you can't make use of your time effectively, you will find yourself overwhelmed by the effort involved.

2 The ability to assert yourself about money. Not only must you know exactly what everything costs, you need to be tough when it comes to haggling for the best price.

3 The ability to market yourself. No one knows who you are and word-of-mouth marketing only kicks in after you have been in business for a while. When you are starting you will need to publicize your new business in every possible way you can.

4 The ability to turn down possible clients. You will need to turn down any client whose proposed deal will cause you more problems or yield less profit than you need to survive. You don't have to take every job offered to you if the time and capital you will need to invest could be better spent on a more profitable client.

5 The ability to fire clients. Your own business is only going to work if you are tough and single-minded. A common problem is the client who does not pay on time. If your business is hand-to-mouth financially, extending un-asked-for credit can be fatal. You will need to be hard-hearted when you tell the client goodbye.

---

* http://www.askamanager.org/

Index

A4 paper 35
Aberdeen 77
Alison Green.............. 178
Amazon 39
ambitions..................... 65
Andy Warhol................ 14
application form ... 27, 30, 41, 43, 70
Bad borrowing........... 169
bankruptcy 20
Bill Gates..................... 14
BMW............................ 56
Bob Hope................... 171
British Airways 147
C++ software............. 146
capitalism................... 177
career sabotage.......... 91
Casablanca................ 155
College of Cardinals... 82
Commencement 2
Conservative Party 52
Cristiano Ronaldo 14
CV 27, 34, 51, 61, 70
database manager ... 144
David Beckham.......... 172
Death Valley 174
Democrat 52
Departments of Health and Defense 145
Edward Kennedy 25
Einstein.......................... 6
entrepreneur 176
Facebook 39, 52
financial literacy 161
Florence 117
formal management structure 94
Francis of Assisi............6
G8 summit..................155
gagging clause 144
Good borrowing 167
Google 39, 58
gossip 81, 86, 87, 90
graduate school 47
Gregory Peck 71
Gucci and Prada 158
Harvard........................32
Hobbies 18
Hong Kong 155
Human Resources 28
IBM...............................39
internships...................42
interview questions 62
interviewees................77
interviewer styles 70
Ivy League 15
Julia Roberts...............14
Julius Caesar..............99
l'esprit d'escalier 134
landscape gardener....55

LinkedIn 54
Mafia..............................96
Malcolm Gladwell 21
Mark Zuckerberg 175
Marla Gottschalk.........68
Martin Luther King 6
math professor............13
MBA............................139
mental readjustment ..10
Microsoft *Windows* 14
Midas touch 12
Military ranks 140
Name recognition 49
Napoleon 99
National Lottery...........13
Niccolo Machiavelli...117
Ocean's Eleven............26
Orville and Wilbur
  Wright.....................177
Oxford..........................32
Perry Mason 72
personal information ..87
Personality...................61
Peter Principle...........110
Power 94
Preparation..................58
Presentation 60
Pride and Prejudice....33
property developer 55
publishing...................176
Punctuality 58
Reagan era..................40
recruitment agency.....28

Republican...................52
restaurant trade.........176
résumé 27, 34, 35, 36, 37,
  43, 56, 61, 65, 72
Retirement, ...17
Richard Branson 12
Richard Moran...........110
Savile Row.................155
Scotland 77
Shakespeare 86
spell checker 35
strengths 65
Sultan of Turkey........144
Ten mistakes 77
The Prince 117
Time magazine 17
time management.......23
Tom Cruise 71
Twitter..........................54
typo 35
Uncle Mort's Hardware
  Store 43
UNESCO......................96
United Kingdom 13
Vatican 82
Wall Street 171
Walmart........................96
Warren Buffet 12
weaknesses.................66
Wikipedia 58
working environment..82
World Wide Web.........31
Yahoo! 58

www.ingramcontent.com/pod-product-compliance
Lightning Source LLC
Chambersburg PA
CBHW071500040426
42444CB00008B/1422